IMAGES
of America

ELECTRIC BOAT
CORPORATION

THE HOLLAND ON THE POTOMAC, 1900. The *Holland* cruises on the Potomac River near Washington, D.C., in the early spring of 1900 during exhibition runs conducted by Electric Boat Company to interest U.S. Navy and government officials in the boat. The demonstrations paid off. On April 11, the stubby 53-foot craft became the first submarine accepted by the U.S. Navy. The purchase price was $150,000. Today a submarine costs more than $2 billion. Regardless of the price, the *Holland* was a technological marvel for its day. For the first time, one vessel contained all the major components needed for successful underwater operations—a dual propulsion system (a combustion engine for surface running, an electric motor for submerged power), separate main and auxiliary ballast systems (large tanks for submerging, small ones for adjusting trim), a fixed center of gravity, a hydrodynamically advanced hull shape (dolphin), and a modern weapons system (torpedoes). The *Holland* could dive safely to 100 feet and stay under for 24 hours. It had a surface range of 1,000 miles at six knots. Submerged, it could log 20 miles at five knots.

On the cover: The world's first nuclear-powered ship, the submarine *Nautilus* (SSN 571), slides into the Thames River at 11:03 a.m. during its launching from Electric Boat Company's south yard on January 21, 1954. The event took on the trappings of a national holiday throughout the area. Schools and businesses were closed. Some 15,000 people crowded into the yard for the historic occasion. (Courtesy of the General Dynamics Electric Boat Corporation.)

IMAGES
of America

ELECTRIC BOAT
CORPORATION

James S. Reyburn

ARCADIA
PUBLISHING

Published by Arcadia Publishing
Charleston, South Carolina

Library of Congress Catalog Card Number: 2006926497

For all general information contact Arcadia Publishing at:
Telephone 843-853-2070
Fax 843-853-0044
E-mail sales@arcadiapublishing.com
For customer service and orders:
Toll-Free 1-888-313-2665

Visit us on the Internet at www.arcadiapublishing.com

To the men and women of Electric Boat.

FIRST OFFICE BUILDING, C. 1911. The first office building at the Groton facility was built in 1911 to support the New London Ship and Engine Company, an Electric Boat subsidiary formed to build diesel engines. Administrative, engineering, and design personnel were all headquartered there. As the company grew, a number of additions were built in the early years of its existence, all of them earmarked for engineering and design forces. Employees throughout the shipyard began referring to it as "the main office building," a label that continued throughout its use. Traditionally, the top-level executives' offices were there and a reception and waiting room was located inside the front entrance. Eventually, as the workforce increased even more and other buildings were built, the building became the administrative center. The gray stucco structure, a longtime company landmark, was torn down in 1997.

CONTENTS

ACKNOWLEDGMENTS

"No man is an island, entire of itself." John Donne's famous words, written in 1623, are as true today as they were then, especially when one is writing a book. A number of people and organizations kept me connected to the mainland, for which I am most grateful.

First, unless otherwise noted, General Dynamics Electric Boat Corporation and the Submarine Force Library and Museum graciously provided all the images appearing in this book.

Wendy Schnur, reference manager at the Mystic Seaport's G. W. Blunt White Library, kindly led me to volumes from which I gleaned valuable information on the yachts and commercial vessels that appear in this book. I thank Dr. Robert Browning, United States Coast Guard historian, for his lightning-fast response to my request for photographs. And my appreciation to my friends Gretchen Grieshaber Higgins and Ed Behney for loaning photographs from their collections.

Wendy Gulley, archivist at the Submarine Force Library and Museum in Groton, was extremely helpful in making available the photographic files of that venerable facility. Two friends and former colleagues warrant thanks: Jim Burbank, an Electric Boat retiree, who tapped his legendary encyclopedic knowledge of the company for the project, and David Tela, senior public affairs specialist at Electric Boat, who also gave research help.

Four other Electric Boat employees deserve special mention. Robert Hamilton, director of communications, paved the way for the project with his support. Barry Black, chief of technical services, opened his historical photographic files. His administrative assistant, Peggy Gleason, was informative and helpful during my research time there. Finally, my deepest thanks and gratitude go to photographer Gary Slater, with whom I worked closely many times at Electric Boat during my tenure there as a news and information specialist. His enthusiasm, commitment, and technical expertise in scanning most of the images for this book were absolutely invaluable.

INTRODUCTION

When Philadelphia entrepreneur Isaac Rice merged two little-known companies on February 7, 1899, to form the Electric Boat Company, many people undoubtedly thought he had finally found a hobby. After all, Rice had already made a sizeable fortune in the electric storage battery field.

But close friends and associates knew better. They were well aware that Rice's only passionate pastime was playing chess and that business was strictly business to him. A brilliant and driven man, he continually sought new challenges. Bringing together the John P. Holland Torpedo Boat Company, which had designed a submarine, and the Electric Launch Company, which built stylish electrically powered launches, offered an excellent opportunity to widen his horizons.

What prompted Rice's decision was a ride he took on July 4, 1898, on the Holland company's submarine *Holland*, which ran submerged on his batteries. While other people were enjoying picnics, parades, and fireworks, Rice was cruising the depths of New York Harbor aboard the cramped and stuffy 53-foot craft. The trip so impressed him that when the small submarine surfaced, Rice resolved to refinance the nearly bankrupt company and build it into profitability.

Rice lost no time in pressing forward with his new venture. In a clever marketing move, he sent the *Holland* to the Potomac River near Washington, D.C., to demonstrate it for U.S. Navy and government officials. Largely as a result of these efforts, the U.S. Navy accepted the *Holland* on April 11, 1900, and ordered more submarines from Electric Boat.

Electric Launch Company's launch business thrived using a method known as "standardized" construction that it had pioneered eight years before building 54 electric-powered launches for the 1893 Chicago World's Fair. The technique called for stockpiling prefabricated sections and parts for later assembly. The company eventually started producing gasoline engine-powered cabin cruisers in the same manner.

Meanwhile, Rice added to the fold the Electro Dynamic Company, which produced small electric motors and generators. Electric Boat prospered. In 1910, the company built a fourth subsidiary, the New London Ship and Engine Company (Nelseco), in Groton, Connecticut, to produce diesel engines for submarines. When Rice died in 1914, he left behind the one of the country's first industrial conglomerates and the now-famous chess opening move the "Rice gambit."

During World War I, Electric Boat built 88 submarines for the U. S. Navy and a number for Britain. Electric Launch Company turned out 722 submarine chasers for Britain, the United States, and several other countries. Electro Dynamic produced thousands of auxiliary electric motors and generators for merchant ships, surface warships, and submarines. By that time, the company had acquired a fourth subsidiary, the Submarine Boat Company, at Port Newark, New Jersey, which produced 118 merchant vessels, the famous Liberty ships.

When World War I ended, Submarine Boat, which finished the remaining 32 ships of the 150-ship contract on its own and began operating them, ran head-on into a postwar shipping slump, and went bankrupt, leaving Electric Boat with a tremendous debt. With no contracts forthcoming for new submarines, the company looked outside the country for work and received a contract for four submarines from Peru. To build those submarines, Electric Boat, which until then had farmed out construction work, enlarged its Nelseco plant at Groton into a shipyard, absorbed Nelseco, and made Electric Launch (renamed Elco) and Electro Dynamic Divisions. In addition, it took on all the commercial work it could get, building yachts, fishing trawlers, ferryboats, tugboats, gunboats, and lighthouse tenders. It also repaired and overhauled vessels.

This work kept the company alive until 1931, when it received the first submarine contract from the U.S. Navy since 1918. The contract was for the *Cuttlefish*, the first partially welded rather than completely riveted submarine and the prototype for the World War II fleet-type submarines. Other orders followed. In 1939, the workforce numbered 2,300. Then the world again went to war. By 1944, the peak year of wartime production, the yard employed more than 12,000 people and was launching a submarine every two weeks. Elco produced 398 motor torpedo boats for the U.S. Navy and Electro Dynamic repeated its World War I performance with its motors and generators.

When World War II ended in 1945, Elco and Electro Dynamic simply resumed their peacetime pursuits. But at Electric Boat's Groton shipyard, the mood was grim. Employment plummeted to 1,200 people. Scrambling to survive, Electric Boat again took on commercial work—fabricating steel for bridges, building fishing trawlers, repairing and overhauling yachts.

But better times were ahead. Lawyer and businessman John Jay Hopkins, the Harvard-educated son of a Fullerton, California, minister, became president of Electric Boat in 1946. That same year, Hopkins engineered the acquisition of Canadair Ltd., Canada's largest aircraft manufacturer, as an Electric Boat subsidiary. Canadair's steady production of aircraft for the Royal Canadian Air Force and a number of commercial airlines helped Electric Boat survive financially until 1951, when the company received the most notable contract in its history—for construction of the world's first nuclear-powered ship, the submarine *Nautilus*. With that contract, Electric Boat became the founding division of General Dynamics Corporation, which in a few years grew into one of the country's largest companies. The one casualty during that time was Elco, which was closed in 1948 when Electric Boat decided to concentrate on submarine construction.

Employment soared at the Groton shipyard to beyond World War II levels. The construction of the early nuclear submarines once again put Electric Boat back on a sound financial footing. During those years, the company became the world's foremost authority on nuclear submarine technology and nuclear propulsion.

In the late 1960s, the company received the contract for the design and construction of the next generation of missile-firing submarines, the Tridents, and received orders to build some ships in the Los Angeles class, the latest fast-attack submarines. Building all 18 Tridents and 33 of the 61 fast-attack submarines kept the shipyard busy until the mid-1990s. In 1993, the company changed its name to the Electric Boat Corporation. After that, it built all three ships in the *Seawolf* fast-attack class. Today the company produces the *Virginia* class of fast-attack submarine, the most sophisticated in the world.

Through the years, Electric Boat has provided a livelihood for tens of thousands of people. For decades, it was the second-largest employer in Connecticut (behind United Technologies) and the largest employer in Rhode Island. Known familiarly as "the Boat," the company has been a major factor in the Rhode Island and Connecticut economies for nearly a century.

This book traces the history of Electric Boat in 217 archival images—through the highs of dizzying success to the lows of near dissolution when little more than Yankee ingenuity kept it alive. Through it all, the company has steadfastly maintained its position at the forefront of submarine technology.

Electric Boat's history is a tale of skilled people producing one of the most complex products ever devised by man—ships that are virtual underwater cities for their crews for months at a time in one of the most hostile environments on earth—inner space. It is a story of designers, engineers, planners, welders, electricians, shipfitters, pipe fitters, and others in a wide range of disciplines who have pooled their talents to turn out a product that continues to be a technological wonder.

One

THE EARLY YEARS

DEBUT OF ELECTRIC LAUNCHES, 1893. The 1893 Chicago World's Fair spotlighted architecture and the wonders of electricity, and Electric Launch Company's 54 electrically powered launches were the hit of the show. The 20-passenger launches plying the fair's lagoons delighted fairgoers with a quiet ride, enabling them to converse in a normal voice. Uniformed launch operators were forever answering the question "Hey mister, how do these things run?" Electric Launch became one of the first units of Electric Boat Company in 1899 along with the Holland Torpedo Boat Company. Continuing to build opulent electric launches for European royalty and wealthy Americans, the company, pioneering standardized construction, began producing a line of power cruisers that became the most emulated craft in that field. It went on to design and build torpedo boats during both world wars. Until 1948, when it closed, Electric Launch was a premier and well-respected name in both civilian and military boatbuilding.

JOHN PHILLIP HOLLAND (1842–1914), c. 1899. Topped by his signature derby, John Phillip Holland peers from the turret of the invention bearing his name, the submarine *Holland*. An Irish immigrant, he taught school in New Jersey while perfecting submarine designs. He crafted five submarines before succeeding with the *Holland*, a feat that earned him the title "Father of the Modern Submarine." Electric Boat Company was founded in 1899 to complete the *Holland*'s sea trials.

ISAAC RICE (1850–1914), c. 1899. On February 7, 1899, entrepreneur and former railroad lawyer Isaac Rice, president of the Electric Storage Battery Company in Philadelphia, formed Electric Boat Company with the joining of the Electric Launch Company (later Elco) and the Holland Torpedo Boat Company. Later adding the Electro Dynamic Company, a builder of electric motors, to the group, Rice built Electric Boat into one of the country's first industrial conglomerates.

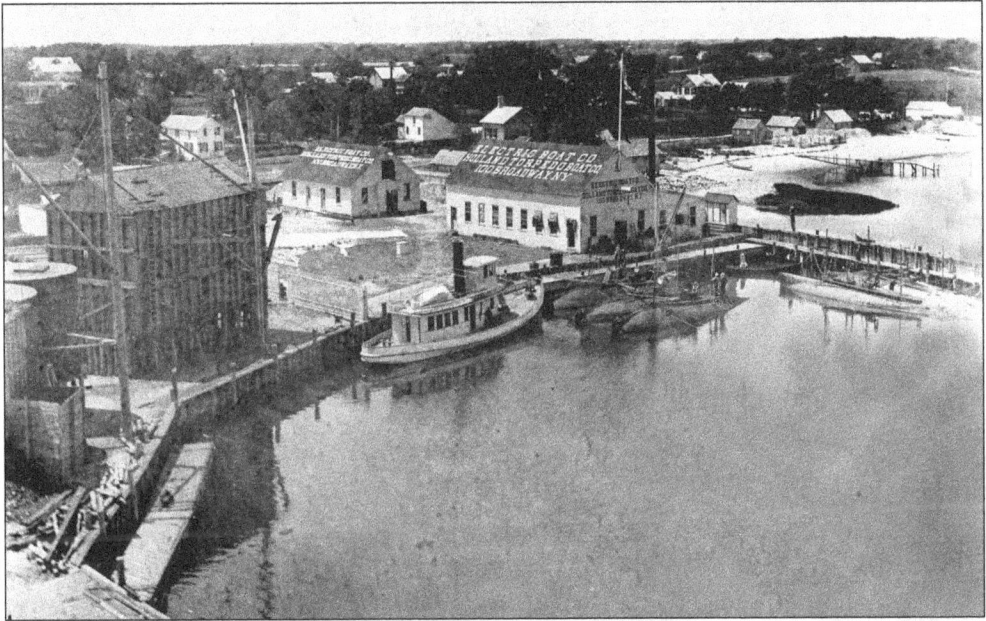

EARLY SEA TRIAL BASE, C. 1899. Concerned with the heavily trafficked New York Harbor as a sea trial area, Electric Boat leased this yard at New Suffolk, New York, on eastern Long Island. Three A boats of the first submarine class are moored at right center. Off their bows is the tender *Kelpie* that served as a tender during seas trials. New Suffolk was the nation's first unofficial submarine base.

YARD EMPLOYEES, C. 1899. A workforce composed mainly of machinists, pipe fitters, and electricians at the Holland Torpedo Boat Company's New Suffolk yard poses for a cameraman alongside a support building. The Holland company at that time still maintained its name and its main office at 100 Broadway in New York City but had become a subsidiary of Electric Boat earlier that year.

INVENTOR AND FRIENDS, 1898. John P. Holland (third from left) and his longtime friend Charles Morris, on his right, stand flanked by two unidentified men before an early set of *Holland* sea trials. Morris, a fellow inventor and superintending engineer on the *Holland* project, had been Holland's employer in the earlier discouraging years.

WILLIAM WOODNUT GRISCOM (1851–1897), C. 1895. William Woodnut Griscom, who had 40 inventions to his credit, founded the Philadelphia-based Electro Dynamic Company, which produced fractional electric motors for sewing machines, in 1880. Electric Boat founder Isaac Rice bought the financially ailing company in 1899, two years after Griscom died in a hunting accident at 46. The company was a part of Electric Boat for 101 years.

CZAR'S LAUNCH, C. 1899. Czar Nicholas II of Russia, apparently impressed with Grand Duke Alexander's electric launch, ordered this 37-foot launch from the Electric Launch Company in 1897. The czar used it as a tender for the imperial yacht *Polar Star*. The czar's fleet captain ordered the launch through the Russian naval attaché in Washington, D.C.

THOUSAND ISLANDS LAUNCH, C. 1899. Electric Launch Company's electric launches were popular at summer resorts. Here, with opulent wicker chairs and plush cushions neatly in place, the launch *Karuna* is readied for a cruise on a waterway in New York's Thousand Islands, where many business magnates of the day owned summer homes.

LARGEST FREIGHTER, C. 1902. In the early 1900s, railroad magnate James J. Hill built two huge steel freight/passenger vessels on the Groton site that Electric Boat would later occupy. Here the *Minnesota*, launched in 1903, takes shape. The *Dakota* followed in 1904. At 622 feet long and 22,250 deadweight tons, they were the largest ships of their time. The *Dakota* struck a reef off Japan in 1907 and sank. The *Minnesota* became a troopship in World War I.

PIER APPROACH, C. 1900. With coiled line in hand and ready to throw, a crewman mans his docking station on the forward deck as the *Holland*, running at dead slow speed, maneuvers for a landing. The man standing behind the open turret is busy giving signals to line handlers ashore and instructions to the crewmen below operating the 45-horsepower Otto gasoline engine used for surface propulsion.

THE *HOLLAND* AT PIER, C. 1900. In another image, most likely taken at the United States Naval Academy at Annapolis, Maryland, some crew members and a few academy midshipmen on board for training gather on the deck of the *Holland* for a group photograph. In the next slip, the smokestack of a steam-driven launch pokes above an awning while two surface monitors appear in the distance.

THE *HOLLAND* AT CRESCENT SHIPYARD, C. 1900. Sporting a fresh coat of paint and with its torpedo port uncovered at the bow, the *Holland* rests on keel blocks at the Crescent Shipyard in Elizabethport, New Jersey, where it was built. The *Holland* displaced 75 tons submerged. By contrast, today's Trident submarines, America's largest, displace 18,750 tons.

DRY DOCK WORK, C. 1900. The *Holland* rests in a dry dock at the New York Navy Yard as workers perform maintenance. This image clearly shows the cigar-shaped hull of the small submarine. The *Holland* had a crew of five that operated the boat in an open but cramped compartment inside. Today's large submarines carry a crew of up to 154 men.

DRAFTSMEN FOR EARLY SUBMARINES, C. 1900. This design team posing in sartorial splendor worked on plans for the *Holland*, the A boats, and other early submarines. The jacketed man at left front was probably the supervisor. Vests, starched collars, and bow ties seemed to be the favored working apparel in those early days.

ELECTRIC LAUNCH, C. 1902. With a professional captain at the helm, the Robert P. Lindeman family enjoys an afternoon cruise off Fishers Island, New York, in their 30-foot electric launch built by the Electric Launch Company. This well-appointed model sported a surrey (then called "fly ash") top, wicker furniture, and carpeted deck. The launch would run for 10 hours at five knots on one charge.

FIRST HOLLAND CREW, 1901. Among the first U.S. Navy crew of the *Holland* posing on board at Newport, Rhode Island, in 1901 are Lt. H. H. Caldwell, the commanding officer (in turret), and warrant gunner Owen Hill (standing, second from right). Gunner's mate first class Harry Wahab (standing at left) fired the first torpedo from the *Holland*, and Hill became the second commanding officer two years later.

SUBMARINE ON BUILDING WAYS, C. 1901. Construction progresses on an early A-class submarine at the Crescent Shipyard in Elizabethport, New Jersey. Circular hull frames are in place awaiting hull plates to cover them. The Crescent yard, which had produced the *Holland*, by that time was a leader in submarine construction.

THE *HOLLAND* AND BATTLESHIP, 1901. With each vessel secured over its respective keel blocks, the *Holland* and the Russian battleship *Retvizan* wait for the graving dock to be pumped out at the Brooklyn (New York) Navy Yard. Curious crews of both vessels peer at one another, perhaps with thoughts of the meeting of David and Goliath. Three years later, Russia bought an Electric Boat submarine.

NEW SUFFOLK ANCHORAGE, C. 1902. In another view of the New Suffolk facility, two early submarines lay moored at the facility's small cove. At center, yard workers perform various chores on the deck of the *Adder* (A-2) while the bow of another A-class submarine appears at right. Support buildings are in the background.

HENRY B. SUTPHEN (1870–1950), C. 1910. Henry B. Sutphen joined Electric Launch Company in 1892 and later became the Elco Division's general manager. Sutphen was appointed an Electric Boat director in 1905, a vice president in 1925, and, in 1942, executive vice president. He was instrumental in the development of submarine chasers and merchant ships in World War I and Elco PT boats in World War II. His career spanned 58 years.

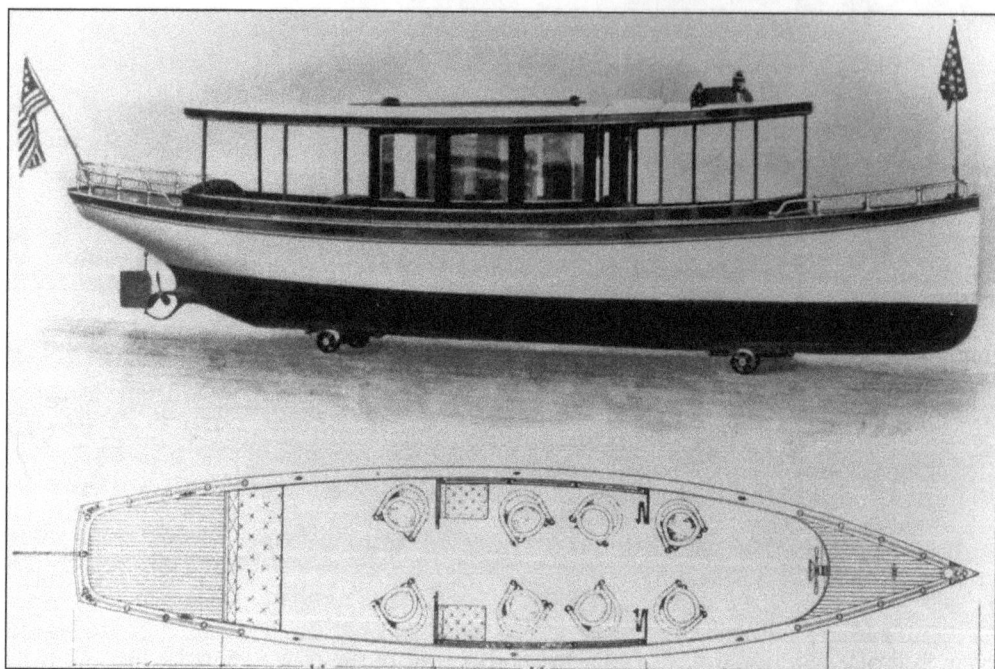

ELCO CATALOG ENTRY, C. 1902. The description of this launch in the catalog read, "New Design, Open cabin, Wide Drop Windows, For Day Excursion. Telescoping or folding doors to easily throw cabin wide open in fair weather. Two built last year . . . Standard construction . . . Finished in mahogany. Standard No. 6 Power Equipment. Price $3,450. Launch, as illustrated, but without deck fittings, FOB cars, our works."

THE *FULTON* CRUISES PECONIC BAY, C. 1904. The *Fulton* plows along in Long Island's Peconic Bay during sea trials. It was sold to the Russian Navy before the Russo-Japanese War (1904–1905). Built in 1901 at the Crescent Shipyard as an experimental prototype for the A boats, it was shipped to Russia on the deck of a freighter under circumstances of great intrigue in 1904 and was renamed *Madam* upon arrival.

FIRST C-CLASS SUBMARINE, C. 1905. The *Octopus*, in dry dock, was the fourth boat built under a 1904 U.S. Navy contract and was the prototype for the C class. Larger and faster than its predecessors, it was 105 feet long, displaced 170 tons submerged, and could dive to 200 feet. The *Octopus* beat rival Simon Lake's *Protector* during competitive sea trials off Rhode Island in 1907, bringing $3 million more in submarine contracts.

SUBMARINES FOR JAPAN, C. 1907. Both sides in the Russo-Japanese War bought Electric Boat submarines. Here six A boats lie moored in Japan in 1907. Frank T. Cable, construction superintendent, led a company team that went to Japan to supervise their assembly, work that he termed "a damned mistake" following the Pearl Harbor attack 37 years later. Cable and his team had been to Russia shortly before, performing the same work.

SUBMARINES READY FOR TRIP, 1909. Looking like strange sea creatures, two Electric Boat–built A-class submarines sit secured on the deck of a freighter in March 1909, ready for shipment to an American naval base in Manila, the Philippines. These submarines were obsolete by 1914 and met a sad end as naval targets in 1922.

MACHINE SHOP, 1910. The New London Ship and Engine Company (Nelseco) machine shop appears in this postcard shortly after being built at Groton, Connecticut. The building, which is still in use today, is framed with steel I beams and the walls are brick. Over the years, the shop has turned out thousands of components for submarines and surface ships.

MACHINE SHOP INTERIOR, C. 1912. This interior view of the machine shop gives a sense of its enormous size. Construction began in 1910, along with that of the foundry and office building. This facility turned out diesel engines for submarines, gasoline engines for Elco-produced submarine chasers, high pressure air compressors, torpedo tubes, conning towers, and periscopes. All this equipment was shipped for installation to the building yards.

RETAINING WALL UNDER CONSTRUCTION, C. 1911. Building the New London Ship and Engine Company facilities required some shoring of the Thames River bank. At left, a retaining wall stands ready for backfilling. The railroad flatcar holds material being used in the project. The powerhouse appears in the background. The land the houses occupied at right was eventually used in a shipyard expansion.

COMPANY DRAFTSMEN, C. 1912. New London Ship and Engine Company draftsmen gather at the front entrance of the office building. The building, which provided sweeping vistas from most offices of the lower Thames River and of New London on the opposite shore, fronted directly on Eastern Point Road, which runs for two miles down the Groton, or east, side of the river.

NEARBY STORE, C. 1912. An unidentified man (perhaps the owner) and his dog pose in front of a small store that operated for many years across Eastern Point Road from the New London Ship and Engine Company office building. The store's convenient location in this busy area was undoubtedly a major factor in its longevity.

NELSECO FOUNDRY, 1911. Like the machine shop and the office building, the New London Ship and Engine Company foundry shown in this postcard was among the first buildings constructed on the Groton site of the former Eastern Shipbuilding Company. Laid out in the general early-20th-century "smokestack" design, the facility produced thousands of castings over the years for all kinds of vessels as well as nonmarine projects.

FOUNDRY PERSONNEL, 1912. Dozens of New London Ship and Engine Company foundry workers pose for the photographer. Even the overhead crane operator (at left), standing in a confident hand-on-hip pose, has stopped his lift of what appears to be a large casting from the foundry floor to be included in the image.

A VIEW LOOKING NORTH, C. 1912. This early view of the New London Ship and Engine Company property looks north near the waterfront. At left is the machine shop. Across the tracks is a house with all its windows removed and its first floor partially torn up, indicating that it was being readied to be moved or demolished. Storehouses later occupied that area.

HOTEL NELSECO, C. 1912. This hotel, built by New London Ship and Engine Company, first named the Olympia and then Hotel Nelseco, provided comfortable quarters for employees and business visitors. It was conveniently located across Eastern Point Road from the company's office building. In 1932, it was remodeled into the office complex for the U.S. Navy's on-site supervisor of shipbuilding.

CONNECTING WALKWAY, C. 1912. A group of employees start down a newly completed long pedestrian bridge built from the company office building, in the background, to the machine shop. The bridge, built of steel supports holding wooden flooring, made the trip easier, safer, and quicker on the dangerously steep hill between the two buildings.

LOWER END OF THE BRIDGE, C. 1912. At the lower end of the bridge was an enclosed elevator tower that gave walkers access to the machine shop. Just beyond the tower is a smaller bridge running between the machine shop and a storehouse. That bridge allowed employees to cross more safely than walking across the railroad tracks and the vehicular thoroughfare at ground level.

NELSECO PLANT, C. 1913. This view of the New London Ship and Engine Company looking south clearly shows the rural landscape on the Groton shore at that time. The machine shop is the building closest to the camera while the office building appears on the hill at the upper left. A four-masted schooner lies at anchor in the middle of the Thames River.

COMPANY BAND, 1913. Surrounding what appears to be a huge cornstalk, the 30-member New London Ship and Engine Company band gathers for a group portrait in front of a large banner marking the company's exhibit at a community fair. Like its descendant, the Electric Boat band pictured on page 73, the band made its presence known at company and community functions with stirring martial music.

MACHINE SHOP, C. 1913. In this view of Groton looking south, a small boatyard appears north of the New London Ship and Engine Company machine shop. Hauled out at the boatyard are a skiff, a sailboat, and several powerboats, some covered for the winter. This area later became part of Electric Boat's north yard.

FIRST DIESEL YACHT, C. 1914. America's first diesel-powered yacht, the elegant 84-foot *Idealia*, was a joint venture of Elco, which built it, and New London Ship and Engine Company, which produced its 120-horsepower four-cycle engine. "Her engine burns fuel oil costing three cents per gallon at New York," reported a company flyer. In 1915, the *Idealia*, owned by Electric Boat, cruised 3,000 miles from New York to Canadian waters and back.

LAWRENCE Y. SPEAR (1870–1950), c. 1914. An 1890 graduate of the United States Naval Academy, Lawrence Y. Spear served 12 years in the U.S. Navy, then joined Electric Boat in 1902 as naval architect and vice president. Spear and John P. Holland clashed often, then became embroiled in a dispute over the automatic controls Holland had insisted upon for his submarines. The showdown came when the diving planes on the C-class *Octopus* jammed, sending the submarine to the bottom. Fortunately the skipper and crew were able to resurface by blowing the ballast tanks. Shortly after that, Spear ordered controls on all boats replaced with manual controls without Holland's knowledge. Furious, Holland accused Spear of ruining "my life's work." When Holland's contract expired in 1904, the inventor resigned. He died in 1914 of pneumonia at his home in Newark, New Jersey. Spear became president of New London Ship and Engine Company in 1911, then president of Electric Boat in 1942, and the company's board chairman in 1947.

Two

WORLD WAR I

"YACHTS" FOR WAR DUTY, C. 1916. These three 75-foot motor launches (MLs) at Elco's plant in Bayonne, New Jersey, were in a group of 50 built for England early in the war for antisubmarine duty at the request of a shipbuilder representing the British government. Because the United States was neutral at the time, they were sent to Canada disguised as yachts, then shipped overseas on the decks of freighters. After the Cunard liner *Lusitania* was sunk on May 7, 1915, the shipbuilder cabled Elco for 500 more launches to be delivered before November 15, 1916, only a year and a half away. Henry B. Sutphen accepted the challenge. Skeptics scoffed, but Irwin Chase, Elco's chief designer, stretched the design to 80 feet and the company, using standardized construction, turned them out in 488 days, well beating the deadline. This astonishing feat put Elco in the shipbuilding record books as an extremely astute company.

ELCO SUBMARINE CHASERS, 1917. Eight 80-foot motor launches (by then called submarine chasers) lie moored in Canada awaiting shipment to Britain. Elco circumvented the neutrality restrictions this time by building the boats in parts at Bayonne and shipping them crated and numbered in 3,000 railroad cars to Montreal, where they were assembled. The completed boats were transported on flatcars to Halifax, Nova Scotia, where they were loaded aboard British freighters and crossed the Atlantic Ocean. The boats served in the North Sea, the English Channel, the Mediterranean Sea, and the Dardanelles on antisubmarine patrols, convoy duty, rescue work, and mine laying and sweeping. Carrying depth charges, they were particularly effective against U-boats, continually surprising and sinking them. In addition to the 550 built for Britain, Elco also produced another 172 for the United States, France, and Italy for a total of 722 vessels, a highly impressive testament to standardized construction.

SUBMARINE CHASER UNDERWAY, C. 1917. Here is an Elco 80-foot submarine chaser underway. Its condition suggests that it has seen heavy use, perhaps in combat in European waters. These vessels, built mainly for and operated by Britain's Royal Navy, carried out persistent attacks on German U-boats, helping to keep vital sea-lanes open for merchant shipping.

H BOATS FOR BRITAIN, C. 1917. In addition to the submarine chasers, Electric Boat built 10 H-class submarines for Britain in Montreal in an astounding 10 months. They served with the Royal Navy in the Baltic and Mediterranean Seas. Britain built 32 more under Electric Boat license. Electric Boat also built a total of 19 H boats for Russia and Italy that saw action in the Baltic and Adriatic Seas.

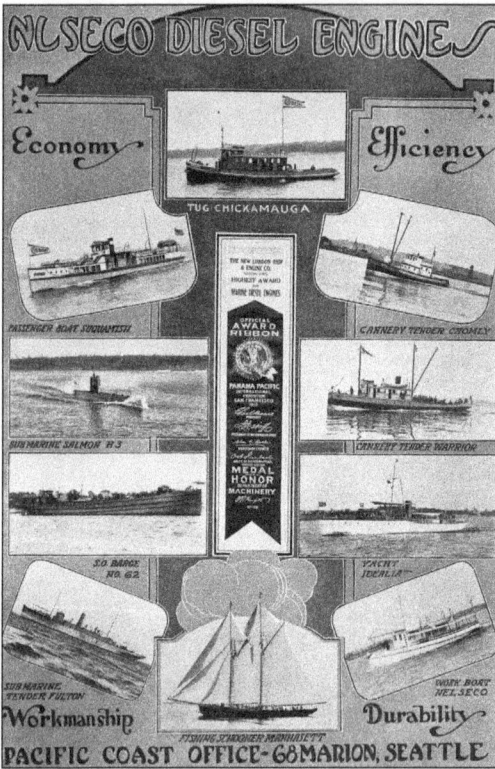

NLSECO DIESEL ENGINES

Economy

Efficiency

TUG CHICKAMAUGA

PASSENGER BOAT SUQUAMISH

CANNERY TENDER CROMEY

SUB MARINE SALMON N 3

CANNERY TENDER WARRIOR

S.D BARGE NO. 62

YACHT IDEALIA

SUB MARINE TENDER FULTON

WORK BOAT NELSECO

Workmanship

Durability

FISHING SCHOONER MANHASETT

PACIFIC COAST OFFICE- 68 MARION, SEATTLE

PRODUCT AND HONORS BANNER, C. 1915. This colorful banner shows the wide variety of vessels powered by New London Ship and Engine Company's diesel engines, which enjoyed an excellent reputation. The ribbon in the center of the banner is the highest award for marine diesel engines at the Panama Pacific International Exposition, held in San Francisco in 1915.

THE *HOLLAND* MOVED FROM MUSEUM, 1916. In 1905, with submarine technology advancing rapidly, the *Holland* was retired. Decommissioned in 1910, it was exhibited at various places, In this image, the last taken of it, a team of horses haul it from a Philadelphia museum prior to a trip to Starlight Park in the Bronx, New York, its last home. It was sold for scrap for $100 in 1932 when the park closed.

SUBMARINE CHASER IN COMBAT, 1918.
An Elco 80-foot submarine chaser in
this poster image puts its bow in the air
as it dusts off a large wave crest while on
antisubmarine patrol. The copy in the
lower right reads, "Hounding the Hun
from the Seas." In the sky above the
chaser is a dirigible used to spot enemy
U-boats from the air.

Hounding
the Hun from
the Seas...

ARMY DREDGE ENGINE, C. 1917. This Nelseco Model 6-MI-18 diesel engine, which generated
350 horsepower at 280 revolutions per minute, was installed in the U.S. Army Corps of Engineers'
dredge No. 1407, yet another application for the popular engines. The two square fittings on the
upper part of the engine are air intake filters.

STATIONARY POWER PLANT ENGINE, C. 1917. In addition to powering ships and boats, New London Ship and Engine Company diesels powered energy plants in a number of locations as well. This 330-horsepower model rumbles along generating power at Napierville, Illinois, while a nattily dressed employee checks its operation. Another company diesel provided energy for the Florida Light and Power plant in Sarasota, among other cities.

GROTON PLANT, 1918. This aerial view shows the Groton facility as it looked a year after the United States had entered World War I. The long building in the center is the machine shop. The powerhouse appears just to right of the machine shop, while the office building appears on the hill at right center. The open land at right center is now occupied by a number of buildings.

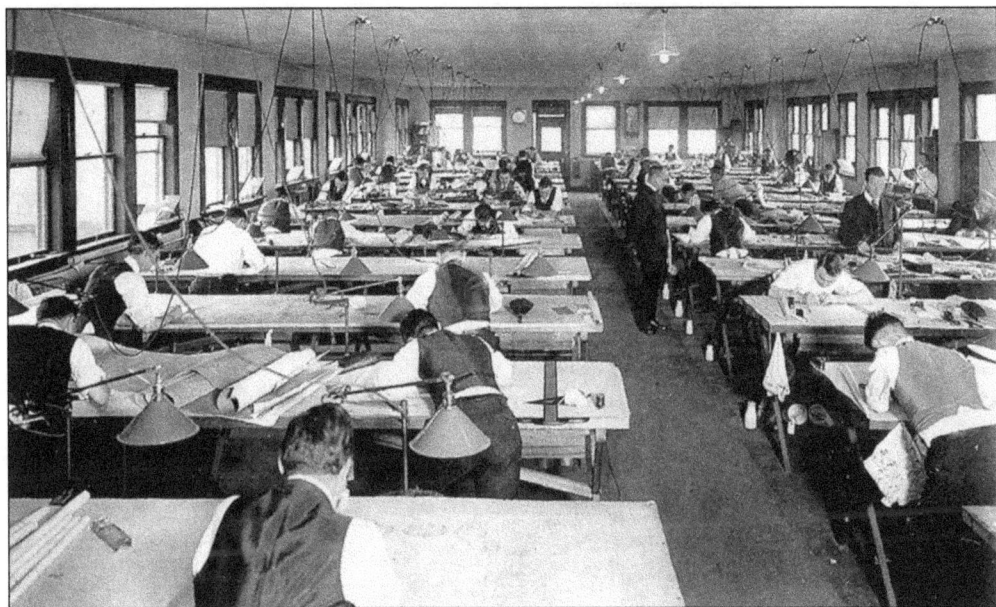

DRAFTING ROOM, 1918. Draftsmen hunch over their tables at the Groton plant focusing on specification drawings. These designers handled thousands of plans detailing complex submarine systems ranging from ballast tanks and engines to piping and wiring. Today Electric Boat designers, working with much more complicated systems, use a quicker method—computers—to design in three dimensions and virtual reality.

SUBMARINE BOAT FACILITY, 1918. In September 1917, the Submarine Boat Company, an Electric Boat subsidiary, began building a shipyard on 35 acres of marsh in Port Newark, New Jersey, to build merchant ships. Within eight months, it had launched its first ship using standardized construction, suggested earlier by Henry B. Sutphen, Elco vice president. Completed ships lie moored in the channel at the left while some ways appear at the lower right.

PARTS AWAIT INSTALLATION, 1918. Windlasses, blowers, steering engines, and boiler parts sit lined up in a storage area at Submarine Boat awaiting installation on Liberty ships. In standardized construction, such equipment was built in shops throughout the country that were specialists in their respective fields and shipped to Port Newark. The yard, which employed more than 16,000 people in its heyday, served mainly as an assembly area.

LIBERTY SHIP LAUNCHED, 1918. The *Agawam*, the first ship produced by Submarine Boat, is launched at Port Newark on May 30, 1918. Built of abundant structural steel rather than scarce ship steel, the 5,500-ton vessel was the first of 118 built by the company during the conflict. When the *Agawam* floated free of the marine railway, a shipyard executive exclaimed, "My God, the damned thing floats!"

THE AGAWAM READY FOR THE ATLANTIC, 1918. Painted in a "dazzle" camouflage motif to confuse enemy ships, the armed *Agawam*, loaded with war cargo, sits in New York Harbor before its first trip across the Atlantic Ocean. The standardized ships were 335 feet long and had a 46-foot beam and five cargo holds. Each was powered by a 1,500-horsepower steam turbine engine, which gave a top speed of 10.5 knots.

ENGINES IN PRODUCTION, 1918. New London Ship and Engine Company built the first diesel engines in America. Here a number are in various stages of construction in the machine shop. Diesels were much safer than gasoline engines and more fuel-efficient. The first submarines to be fitted with the new engines were some of the E class, which then crossed the Atlantic under their own power with no breakdowns.

MILLING MACHINE, 1918. A New London Ship and Engine Company machine operator turns a large casting in a sizeable milling machine. In his left hand he holds a micrometer he will use to measure the diameter of the piece periodically. During World War I, New London Ship and Engine Company turned out equipment for submarines, surface warships, and cargo vessels.

FERRYBOAT GOVERNOR WINTHROP, C. 1918. The ferryboat *Governor Winthrop* heads across the Thames River on its run from New London to Groton. Many New London Ship and Engine Company and Electric Boat employees commuted on this and other ferries, which ran for years on the one-mile route. Ferry service ended in 1929, when automobiles became the favored form of transportation.

Three

BETWEEN THE WARS

ELCO 50-FOOTER, 1920. Showing the classic features of post–World War I Elco cruisers—the plumb bow and the two-level deck line inspired by Elco's World War I submarine chasers—this 50-footer also has a high "stand-up" canopy, allowing the helmsman to stay in out of the weather. Later Elco cruisers, built in the late 1920s and early 1930s, had much the same classic lines, and some are still cruising today. Most of these cruisers, prized as collector's items, are maintained in "Bristol" fashion by their proud owners, most of whom are members of Port Elco, an elite club of Elco owners formed many years ago. The vintage Elcos have labor-intensive wooden hulls in this age of fiberglass boats, and most still are powered by their original gasoline engines. The challenge for owners, of course, is to find a good yard that can handle both the wooden hulls and the gasoline engines.

CANAL BARGE, 1921. When World War I ended in November 1918, Submarine Boat finished the 32 ships remaining on the 150-ship contract on its own and began operating them as Transmarine Corporation. A shipping slump brought severe losses. In a turnaround effort, the company operated 16 of these 400-ton barges on the Erie Canal. The effort failed, bankrupting Submarine Boat. It took Electric Boat seven years to recover financially.

S BOATS ARRIVE FOR RENOVATION, 1923. In 1922, Electric Boat received a contract to overhaul 30 S-class submarines built during World War I. Here three of those boats, from left to right, the S-18, S-47, and S-44, lay moored beside a floating machine shop at Groton. The contract prompted Electric Boat, which until then had subcontracted all construction and overhaul work to other yards, to establish a shipyard at Groton.

NEW MARINE RAILWAY, 1923. To handle the overhaul work, Electric Boat built a marine railway. Here the *S-39* undergoes overhaul at Groton. Before then, such work was subcontracted to the Thames Shipyard, several miles up the Thames River. At best, the arrangement had been costly and inefficient, especially during cold weather, when ice in the river hindered submarine movement.

ELCO OPENS IN MANHATTAN, 1923. Spurred by increasing sales brought about in part by its introduction of installment buying three years earlier, Elco borrowed an idea from the automobile industry and opened this showroom in New York City. Prospective customers could walk in, inspect a range of boats, and talk with sales representatives. The marketing drew good results until the Depression, which hit Elco hard.

S BOAT SPONSOR, 1923. Holding a large bouquet of flowers, Mrs. Hugo Grieshaber poses with a champagne bottle before christening the submarine *S-44* at Bethlehem Shipbuilding Corporation's Fore River, Massachusetts, shipyard, on October 27, 1923. Mrs. Grieshaber was the wife of Electric Boat designer Hugo Grieshaber, who appears in the photograph on page 16 standing second from right. (Courtesy of Gretchen Grieshaber Higgins.)

THE S-44 LAUNCHING, 1923. Seconds after Mrs. Greishaber christened the vessel, the *S-44* slid into the Fore River at Quincy, Massachusetts. Before the mid-1920s, Bethlehem Shipbuilding at Fore River built many of the Electric Boat–designed submarines. Later the yard became the Quincy Shipbuilding Division of General Dynamics and built liquefied natural gas tankers, maritime pre-positioning ships, and other large surface vessels. (Courtesy of Gretchen Grieshaber Higgins.)

FRANK T. CABLE (1863–1945), C. 1920.
An outstanding figure in early submarine
development, Frank T. Cable joined the
Holland Torpedo Boat Company in 1897.
Early in his career, Cable commanded
the *Holland* during its sea trails and
trained crews on the early Electric Boat
submarines. He selected the Groton site
of the New London Ship and Engine
Company and was general manager there
for 18 years.

NELSECO-POWERED FERRIES, C. 1924. These double-ended ferries, which operated across Long
Island Sound between Port Washington and New Rochelle, New York, were each powered
by two New London Ship and Engine Company Model 6-MI-18 diesel engines. Each engine
generated 350 brake horsepower at 280 revolutions per minute. The company's engines also
powered freighters, trawlers, yachts, and tugboats. Such commercial work was quite helpful for
the shipyard.

MID-1920S CONSTRUCTION PROJECTS, 1926. With no U.S. Navy new-construction contracts forthcoming following World War I, Electric Boat turned to foreign markets for submarine work. Peru ordered four R-class submarines in 1923, and the company enlarged its Groton plant to build them. Here the Peruvian submarines *R1* and *R2* are under construction alongside the ferryboat *Elmer W. Jones* (left), one of four ferryboats built at Groton from 1926 to 1929.

FIRST GROTON-BUILT SUBMARINES, 1926. The Peruvian boats were the first submarines built at Groton by Electric Boat. Before then, the company had subcontracted all construction work to other shipyards. Here the *R-2* slides into the Thames River on April 29, 1926, as yard workers and some crew members watch from the deck and conning tower. The New London shoreline appears in the background.

46

ANOTHER PRODUCT, C. 1926. Both the B. M. *Thomas*, a tug owned by the Warner Company of Philadelphia, and its engine, a New London Ship and Engine Company Model 6-MIR-22, were built by Electric Boat. The steel-hulled B. M. *Thomas* was 82 feet long and displaced 140 tons. It was built in 1926.

TUGBOAT, C. 1927. The cook (in white) apparently stepped out onto the deck from his galley just in time to join another crew member on the stern to get into the picture of this handsome 86-foot tug *Lone Star*, which was powered by a 530-horsepower New London Ship and Engine Company diesel engine. The *Lone Star* was built in 1927 in Newburgh, New York, for the Lone Star Cement Company.

CRAFTING A CRANKCASE, 1928. In this image, six machinists work side by side assembling a huge crankcase for a New London Ship and Engine Company diesel engine under the watchful eye of a foreman (right). The crankcase became part of the giant engine in the image below. The connection for the propeller shaft appears at left.

GIANT DIESEL ENGINE, 1928. Dwarfing its operators, this huge 3,680-horsepower diesel engine was built by New London Ship and Engine Company at Groton. The engine ran faultlessly during a 30-day test run. Under license from a German firm, New London Ship and Engine built the first marine diesel engines in the United States. Six E-class submarines were fitted with them in the 1920s.

MOTOR SHIP WILSCOX, C. 1929. Electric Boat repowered this 401-foot, 5,900-ton freighter, the MS *Wilscox*, with the huge diesel engine pictured at the bottom of page 48. Originally steam-powered, the *Wilscox* was one of many merchant ships owned by the United States Shipping Board at that time and was operated by the Roosevelt Steamship Company. It was built in 1919 in Tampa, Florida, by the Oscar Daniels Company.

YACHT BEING OVERHAULED, C. 1929. Looking like a small ocean liner, the huge yacht *Utowana* rests on Electric Boat's marine railway undergoing overhaul. The *Utowana* was 230 feet long and displaced 690 tons. The yard performed many such yacht overhauls to keep its doors open when naval work was slow. Later Sir Thomas Lipton brought his America's Cup contender, the magnificent J boat *Shamrock V* back year after year for refurbishing.

POSSIBLE SMALL CUSTOMER, C. 1929. Moored at a dock off the starboard quarter of the *Utowana* is the auxiliary cutter *Venture*, also of New York. Its furled sails indicate that it may have just arrived at the yard. Its owner, Alden Smith of Oyster Bay, New York, might have been there just for a visit to the *Utowana* or possibly for repairs or an overhaul.

IN FOR RIGGING WORK, C. 1930. The stately 147-foot auxiliary brig *Illyria* came to the shipyard for rigging repairs. The yacht, designed by Henry Gielow and built in Lussinpiccolo, Italy, in 1928, belonged to Cornelius Crane of Ipswich, Massachusetts, and was registered in Gloucester, Massachusetts. The range of commercial work Electric Boat performed in those days made the facility what is termed a "full-service" shipyard.

LIGHTHOUSE TENDER, 1930. In still more commercial work, Electric Boat built two lighthouse tenders for the United States Lighthouse Service. Here crew members of the first tender, the 120-foot *Althea*, launched on February 24, 1930, hook up a piling for hauling off a beach. In 1939, the *Althea* became a Coast Guard vessel when that service absorbed the lighthouse service. (Courtesy of the United States Coast Guard.)

THE POINCIANA READY FOR LAUNCH, 1930. Bedecked with flags and pennants, the *Poinciana*, the second lighthouse tender built by Electric Boat and a sister ship of the *Althea*, sits ready for launching on June 30, 1930. Like the *Althea*, the *Poinciana* served in the United States Coast Guard after 1939. Both ships were sold to private interests in the 1960s and operated into the 1970s. (Courtesy of the United States Coast Guard.)

STEEL SLOOP WELDERA, 1932. No boat was too small for Electric Boat to build during the years between World Wars I and II. In this image, taken on June 10, 1932, the *Weldera*, an all-steel, 28-foot sloop, takes shape on the building ways. The *Weldera* displaced 7,000 pounds, drew eight-and-a-half feet, and was a respected competitor in local races for many years.

SCHOONER PURITAN, 1933. The *Puritan*, a striking 102-foot John Alden–designed schooner, was one of several yachts built by Electric Boat's Groton yard during the lean years in the late 1920s and early 1930s. Its owner sailed it out of Newport Beach, California. Appropriated by the U.S. Navy during World War II, it made antisubmarine patrols off Mexico. At last check, the *Puritan* was registered in the English Channel island of Jersey and still sailing. (Author's collection.)

CUTTLEFISH AWAITS LAUNCHING, 1934. Adorned with colorful bunting, the *Cuttlefish* (SS 171) awaits its launching on June 8, 1934. The *Cuttlefish* was the first American submarine built at Groton, ending a 13-year drought of U.S. Navy contracts. It was also the first submarine with a partially welded rather than a completely riveted hull and was a prototype for the World War II fleet-type submarines.

MUNITIONS INVESTIGATION, 1934. From left to right, Henry B. Sutphen, Lawrence Y. Spear, and Electric Boat president Henry Carse sit at the right of microphones during a Senate committee investigation in Washington, D.C., into munitions manufacturing. One of few U.S. companies with foreign business during World War I, Electric Boat was singled out as a whipping boy. Eventually the company was cleared of charges of "excessive profiteering," but not before its records were searched.

FUTURE YARD, C. 1938. The shipyard in this aerial view became Electric Boat's victory yard early in World War II. During and just after World War I, the Union Iron Works had produced freighters there. Like Electric Boat subsidiary Submarine Boat, the postwar shipping slump bankrupted the company in the early 1920s. The three large structures in the center were elevated platforms used as walkways during construction of the large ships.

HOSPITAL TAKES SHAPE, C. 1939. The steel framework for the Electric Boat hospital building reaches skyward as construction proceeds. A mason on the platform at right works on the brick wall, while a steelworker on the building's second level works on the floor. The building, still operating today, is a fully staffed outpatient facility and lies just north of the machine shop (left).

Four

WORLD WAR II

SOUTH YARD START, 1940. The German Luftwaffe and Britain's Royal Air Force were locked in the fateful Battle of Britain when construction crews started clearing the site in September 1940 for Electric Boat's south yard. The new yard, which cost $5 million, added three more building ways to the eight existing in the nearby north yard. The facility opened in June 1941, with the keel laying for the *Barb* (SS 220).

O. POMEROY ROBINSON JR. (1891–1956), C. 1952. O. Pomeroy Robinson Jr., whose career spanned more than 30 years at Electric Boat, served as assistant general manager of the Groton plant, then, as general manager, was responsible for the company's tremendous output during World War II. A Cornell-educated engineer, Robinson was elected a director in 1942, became a vice president in 1943, and a senior vice president early in 1952.

GATO OUTFITTING, 1941. This view of the Groton yard in the summer of 1941 shows the *Gato* (SS 212) undergoing outfitting (center). The *Gato's* design was one of two fleet-type submarine designs frozen early in the war to facilitate speedy production. The other was the design for the *Balao* (SS 285). The *Gato* was the first new Groton-built submarine to join the fleet after the United States entered the war.

FULL PARKING LOT, C. 1943. A sea of vehicles fills a parking lot near Electric Boat, which appears in the background. Wartime gasoline rationing and a shortage of rubber for tires required employees to carpool as much as possible. Company-provided bus transportation to and from outlying communities also took a great number of cars off the road.

STACKED HULL FRAMES, 1943. Submarine hull frames lay stacked ready for placement on building ways in the north yard. The huge gantry cranes in the background were two of several that rolled on tracks in all three Electric Boat yards at Groton. They worked in conjunction with overhead cranes, which operated above the building ways, to move components into position for assembly.

LOWERING A HULL FRAME, 1943. Standing on staging erected high inside hull frames of a submarine taking shape, a worker signals the operator of a crane lowering a frame into place. The frames, set several feet apart, formed the skeleton of the submarine. In later stages of construction, rolled hull plates were welded to the outside of the frames, forming a rigid shell.

ROLLING HULL PLATING, C. 1943. A workman uses a template to check curve accuracy as a machine rolls a steel plate to be used in a submarine hull. The section was then transported to the building ways and welded into a preassigned position as part of the hull. Prefabricating sections like these sped construction because individual plates did not have to be cut and fitted on the building ways.

HULL PLATE INSPECTION, C. 1943. Rolled steel plates are lined up in the shipyard ready to undergo inspection by two U.S. Navy men before being numbered for positioning as part of a submarine hull. The steel was specially formulated to withstand tremendous pressure during deep dives. World War II submarines could descend to more than 400 feet.

SAFETY POSTERS, 1943. Employee safety is always a prime concern at shipyards. At Groton, this sign exhorted workers to do just about everything safely. Other signs kept score on departmental standings in a safety contest. Such posters helped the safety department drive down accident rates per 100 employees from a high of 67 percent in 1941 to 11.2 percent in 1945.

9 E.B.CO. SUBS. HAVE BEEN LOST IN ACTION

GRUNION PERCH SEALION PICKEREL GRAMPUS SHARK AMBERJACK DORADO CORVINA

WE CAN'T REPLACE THE MEN, BUT--- WE CAN REPLACE THE BOATS. **LET'S GO!**

PRODUCTION POSTER, 1943. Posters like this were up all over the Groton shipyard during the war. This one even listed the names of the nine Electric Boat–built submarines that had been lost in action up to that time. Other posters trumpeted such forceful reminders as Keep 'Em Sliding!, which was Electric Boat's motto throughout the war, and the well-known Loose Lips Sink Ships.

WOMEN WELDERS, C. 1943. Well suited-up for their work, three female welders stride confidently toward the photographer in this image taken at Groton. The three were among the 3,000 women hired by the company during the conflict. Electric Boat trained the welders at facilities in Groton and Norwich, about 15 miles north of the yard.

CUTTING STEEL, 1943. Wearing tinted goggles to protect her eyes from the damaging glare of the cutting torch, one tradeswoman trims a small piece of steel at Groton as a colleague stands nearby. Like other defense plants, Electric Boat had women working alongside men at the yard. "One of the women who worked for me was the best electrician in my group," recalled a supervisor years later.

SHIPS' PATCHES, 1943. Ships' patches, usually displaying animated characters, were a morale booster and a source of great pride to crews and yard workers. The upper patch of the *Torsk* (SS 473) shows the submarine breaking an enemy vessel in half while the *Bluegill* (SS 242) patch below shows an angry looking namesake hurling a torpedo. The *Torsk*, still afloat today, is a museum ship at Baltimore's Inner Harbor.

DISNEY CREATIONS, 1943. The Walt Disney Studios created patches for many ships and airplanes. Here the *Crevalle* (SS 291) patch has Pluto, torpedo in hand, charging into the fray on the back of a snarling bulldog. The *Becuna* (SS 319) patch shows a fierce fish unleashing a torpedo under the words "Tiger of the Sea."

TIGHTENING A BOLT, 1943. A shipfitter working with a large wrench tightens a bolt on a submarine section taking shape in front of a nearly completed submarine on the ways. On its wartime footing, the yard was open around the clock seven days a week with three eight-hour shifts daily. In the wartime economic boom, most hourly employees were making more money than they ever had before.

MOVING A HULL SECTION, 1943. To boost submarine production even higher, Electric Boat supervised construction of 28 submarines at Manitowoc Shipbuilding Company in Manitowoc, Wisconsin, during the war. Here a tracked vehicle moves a submarine hull section to an assembly area at that shipyard. The circular area in the center of the section is the pressure hull. Surrounding that is the outer hull shell, which contains ballast tanks.

SIDEWAYS LAUNCH, C. 1943. One of the Manitowoc submarines splashes into the Manitowoc River in a dramatic broadside launch. The river was too narrow to allow the usual lengthwise launchings. A young U.S. Navy ensign who later became an engineer at Electric Boat rode in the conning tower on one such launch. "It was like going over Niagara Falls in a barrel," he reported.

63

FLOATING DRYDOCK, C. 1943. Another Manitowoc submarine sits like a beached whale in a specially designed floating drydock awaiting transport down canals and the Mississippi River to New Orleans, Louisiana, where the submarine proceeded under its own power to its duty station. Parts of that long route were too shallow for the submarines to make the trips on their own. Surfaced, the submarines drew too much. The dry dock drew only six feet.

TORPEDO BOAT LAUNCHING, C. 1943. Scores of spectators watch a specially designed twin-boomed crane lower an 80-foot patrol torpedo boat (PT) into the water following its christening at Elco's Bayonne, New Jersey, yard. The crane was the most efficient way to launch the boats because they were built on a level production line, not on inclined ways.

MODERN WOODWORKING, c. 1943. A jigsaw operator at the Elco Division in Bayonne cuts out an interior component for later installation in a PT. Elco's plant, like all Electric Boat yards, boasted the latest electrically powered woodworking and metalworking machines available. Such equipment assured quick and trouble-free production, an invaluable element when turning out products on a challenging wartime schedule.

Torpedo Boat on Sea Trials, c. 1943. An Elco 80-foot PT boat roars along on sea trials off the New Jersey coast. Elco built 388 PTs, which served mainly in the Pacific theater during World War II. Heavily armed, the PTs, usually operating at night, swept in on their prey with engines muffled, then launched torpedoes from tubes on the deck and sped away. The most famous skipper of an Elco 80-foot PT was Lt. John F. Kennedy, who later became president.

Another well-known person who served on PTs was movie actor Robert Montgomery. The PTs were powered by three 4,050-horsepower Packard gasoline engines that gave a top speed of 41 knots, making these boats the fastest in the war. Although some survived and became yachts, most PTs were burned on South Pacific island beaches after the war to save the cost of transporting them back to the United States.

SHIPFITTER AT WORK, C. 1943. A determined-looking shipfitter reaches inside a submarine component on building ways at Groton's north yard to check for a snug fit on adjoining pieces of steel. Shipfitters, important people in the assembly process, made sure different precut parts of the ship came together properly during construction. The badge on his cap is his union button.

ARTWORK ON CRANES, C. 1943. Prominently displayed on gantry cranes at Groton is a poster depicting a cobia, namesake fish of a submarine under construction, with an enemy ship in its mouth. Such posters boosted morale and reminded workers in a somewhat lighthearted way why they were building ships at a breakneck pace. Until the nuclear age, all submarines were named for fish.

ENDURING HIGH TEMPERATURES, 1944. Shirtless in the heat, two workers weld a flange onto a bullnose used for towing. Like many other components, bullnoses were built on an assembly-line basis and later lifted into position on a submarine's bow. Most construction areas were outside, so employees had to endure a wide range of seasonal temperatures, which at Groton could be extremely high in the summer and bitterly cold in the winter.

LUNCHTIME ENTERTAINMENT, C. 1944. Dozens of employees at Groton gather to watch lunchtime entertainers perform on a makeshift stage set up in front of the plant hospital. The music was a break in an awards program held to present war bonds to winners of a contest to suggest ways to cut lost time. In addition, the company had a suggestion program to encourage shaving production costs.

SOFTBALL GAME, 1944. A pitched ball comes toward a crouched batter ready to hit away as a crowd looks on during a hotly contested lunch-hour softball game at Groton. Sports afforded some relaxation for both participants and spectators and were a good tension breaker in the highly charged atmosphere of wartime production.

YARD RAILROAD, C. 1944. One of three locomotives at the Groton plant pulls a boxcar on a stretch of the yard's nine miles of track. Powered by a Cummins diesel engine, this locomotive, the largest in the yard, could haul 10 to 15 cars. The engineer was a New Haven Railroad veteran. A brakeman stands on the front of the engine while another crewman rides the boxcar's ladder.

HAULING JOB, C. 1944. The big locomotive hauls a flatcar past the north yard fabricating shop and building ways. The shack to the right under the overhead craneways was the yard foremen's headquarters. Behind the staging with men on top at the left are submarines in various stages of construction. This busy scene was typical of the war years.

TYPICAL WARTIME SUBMARINE, 1944. The *Gato*-class *Hake* (SS 256) displaced 1,525 tons and was 307 feet long. Powered by two General Motors diesels on the surface and electric motors submerged, the *Gato* carried a crew of 65–74 and had 10 torpedo tubes, a three-inch deck gun, and a 20-millimeter Oerlikon. Electric Boat built 40 of the 63 *Gato*-class ships, 31 at Groton and 9 at Manitowoc. The cost per ship was $16 million.

ELCO AND ELECTRO DYNAMIC PLANTS, 1944. This artist's rendering shows the Bayonne plants of Elco (foreground) and Electro Dynamic as they appeared during the war. In front of the Elco yard are two large mooring coves sheltered by breakwaters. The Electro Dynamic plant is to the left of the water tower in the background. Both plants were at peak production capacity throughout the war.

ELECTRO DYNAMIC OUTPUT, 1944. Generators are lined up, ready for the next step in production at Electro Dynamic's plant. The unit mass-produced thousands of auxiliary electric motors and generators for merchant vessels, surface warships, and submarines, including all submarines built by Electric Boat. Later, during the nuclear era, Electro Dynamic produced pipe hangers for submarines.

FINISHING DOORWAY, 1944. A shipfitter applies trim on a doorway of a submarine during the fitting out period at a wet dock in Groton. Such detail projects generally were among the last tasks performed shortly before submarines went on sea trials, were delivered, commissioned into the fleet, and sent on their first patrols.

ELECTRIC BOAT BAND, C. 1944. In a lighthearted moment, a drum majorette strikes a marching pose in front of appreciative members of the Electric Boat band. Composed of employees, the band was active during the war and in the immediate postwar years and specialized in stirring John Philip Sousa march tunes. The group performed at special company events, marched in parades in surrounding communities, and gave concerts periodically.

KEEL BLOCKS AWAIT SUBMARINE, C. 1944. High keel blocks for the *Blenny* (SS 324) are in place on building ways awaiting hull frames to be dropped into position on them to extend the small hull section at the rear into a full submarine. With the speedy construction, the remaining frames were probably in position within the next several days. A bullnose (left foreground) lies ready for installation on the submarine's bow. Just after a completed submarine was launched, yard workmen set up the ways so construction could start on another ship almost immediately. Electric Boat used the time-honored method of building submarines and launching them on inclined ways for the last time on September 24, 1994, when fast-attack submarine *Columbia* (SSN 771) slid down the ways. From then on, the yard has launched ships from its land level construction facility.

HOLLYWOOD VISITOR, C. 1944. Movie star Charles Bickford takes a break from a war bond rally to sign autographs for admirers. Bickford was one of several well-known film luminaries to visit the yard during the war. Employees responded enthusiastically to the rallies, buying so many bonds that the company flew the *T* flag of the United States Treasury Department awarded to defense plants that oversubscribed to the drives.

HOMEWARD BOUND

The Seasons Greetings

WARTIME CHRISTMAS CARD, C. 1944. This Electric Boat Christmas card, entitled "Homeward Bound" and executed by an unidentified artist, featured a fleet-type submarine heading to port after a patrol. On the afterdeck are two crewmen gazing at the star of Bethlehem while a red, white, and blue banner waves overhead.

SUBMARINE UNDERGOES FINAL OUTFITTING, 1944. Workers swarm over a fleet-type submarine during final outfitting at Electric Boat's victory yard. This yard, with 10 building ways, was a mile down the Thames River from the south yard, which appears in the distance. Submarines were outfitted in the water at what are still called wet docks, like this one, after they were launched. America's entry into the war after the Pearl Harbor attack on December 7, 1941, was what triggered Electric Boat's acquisition of the victory yard, a shipyard that had produced freighters during World War I. The victory yard nearly doubled Electric Boat's production capacity from 11 to 21 building ways. The facility opened on July 22, 1942, with keel-laying ceremonies for the *Dace* (SS 247). Thousands attended the event, which was aired live on national network radio. Construction of the yard cost $9.5 million. (Author's collection.)

76

ELCO DIVISION PT CONSTRUCTION, 1944. Patrol Torpedo Boat hulls move forward on the production line at the Elco plant at Bayonne. Using a unique construction method, Elco built the laminated mahogany hulls upside down, as shown in this image, then turned them over to insert the engines and install the bulkheads, decks, pilothouses, and armament.

COMMUNITY CHEST POSTER, 1944. Electric Boat employees have always given generously to community organizations. They exceeded the goal set in this campaign for the forerunner of the United Way. Today the company has an employee giving program that donates thousands of dollars each year to local organizations. Employees also give blood on periodic Red Cross drives each year at the shipyard.

RECORD HOLDER, 1945. Crew members pose proudly late in the war at the conning tower of the Electric Boat–built *Flasher* (SS 249), which held the record for tonnage sunk (100,231) during the conflict. Another Electric Boat submarine, the *Tautog* (SS 199), achieved the record for the greatest number (26) of enemy ships sunk. Groton-built submarines accounted for 39 percent of all Japanese ships sunk—1,178 merchant vessels and 218 warships.

WARTIME LAUNCH, 1945. With U.S. Navy and yard personnel on deck, the fleet-type submarine *Cusk* (SS 345) slides into the Thames River at Groton on July 28, 1945, from one of Electric Boat's 21 building ways. The *Cusk* was 1 of 74 submarines built by Electric Boat during World War II. In 1944, the peak year of production, 12,466 employees sent a submarine into the water every two weeks. World War II ended two weeks after the *Cusk* was launched so it never saw action. Employment at Electric Boat had started to decline at the end of the banner production year when the U.S. Navy, with Allied victory assured, had already begun to cancel submarine construction orders. By the end of the war eight months later, submarine output at Electric Boat had slowed to a trickle, and company management had started planning for another bleak period.

Five

THE IMMEDIATE POSTWAR YEARS

SUBMARINE CONVERSION PROJECT, C. 1946. After World War II, the shipyard received a U.S. Navy contract to streamline eight submarines. The Greater Underwater Propulsion Program (GUPPY) involved installing a snorkel, which allowed a submarine's diesel engines to "breathe" while recharging batteries without the submarine having to surface; rounding off the bow; enclosing the chariot bridge; and removing raised deck structures to increase submerged speed. Here is the submarine *Halfbeak* (SS 352) after conversion. The snorkel, a Dutch invention developed by Germany during World War II, began appearing on U-boats late in the war. It eliminated the submarine's Achilles' heel—being caught on the surface by enemy aircraft. Although the device was a major step forward in submarine warfare, it came too late for the Kriegsmarine, which had lost the war at sea by 1943. The postwar GUPPY program led to a new class of submarine employing all the program's features. Electric Boat built a number of them.

ELCO EXPRESS CRUISER, 1946. Showing the influence of patrol torpedo boat design in its curved bow and streamlined superstructure, a sleek postwar Elco 40-foot express cruiser goes through its paces. Shortly after the war, Elco resumed pleasure boat production and offered a full line of power cruisers of advanced design, most of them in the 25 to 40-foot range.

POSTWAR ELCO YACHT, C. 1948. Showing much of the same streamlined features as the 40-footer in the image above, the *Tonya III*, an Elco 60-footer, charges along over calm water with a bone in its teeth. This vessel was one of the few larger yachts the division produced. The owner's private pennant flies from the bow flagstaff while a yacht club burgee flutters from the mainmast. (Author's collection.)

ELCOWOOD MAKES DEBUT, 1946. A Chrysler Town and Country and a Plymouth station wagon, both clad with Elcowood, are parked at Elco's Bayonne plant in 1946. Laminated by high-frequency electrical heat and combining light weight and tremendous strength, Elcowood grew out of Elco's work with patrol torpedo boat construction during World War II. Although it was a promising product, a market never developed. (Courtesy of Ed Behney.)

VALVE INSPECTION, C. 1948. This three-ton cast steel check valve undergoes final inspection in Electric Boat's machine shop before being shipped to the southwest for installation in a natural gas pipeline running between El Paso, Texas, and southern California. This valve and others were machined to tolerances of within two-tenths of a thousandth of an inch.

TALL SHIP OVERHAUL, 1947. The United States Coast Guard training barque *Eagle* undergoes an overhaul on Electric Boat's marine railway at Groton. The majestic 295-foot German ship was taken as a war prize after World War II and was sailed across the Atlantic Ocean by a part-German and part–U. S. Coast Guard crew. Built in Bremerhaven, Germany, in 1936, the *Eagle* was originally named the *Horst Wessel*, after a friend of Adolph Hitler who was killed during a Nazi street rally in Munich in the early 1920s. It was used throughout the war as a sail training ship for German naval cadets. The *Eagle*, which now sails in the place of honor in the lead of tall ship gatherings in this country, is known as "America's Tall Ship." Homeported across the river from Groton in New London at the United States Coast Guard Academy, the *Eagle* still serves as a seagoing classroom for Coast Guard cadets today.

COVERED ELCO BOAT BASIN, 1947. Four models of the 1947 Elco pleasure boat fleet lay moored at piers inside the same enclosed steam-heated boat basin that was used during World War II for patrol torpedo boat outfitting at the Bayonne yard. It was here that the workers installed instruments and other equipment in the boats. The large electrically operated doors at left gave access to open water.

AUTOMATIC PIN-SETTING MACHINE, 1947. Another product Electric Boat developed in the postwar years was this automatic bowling pin–setting machine. The device set up the pins after each frame. To go with the machine, the Elco Division built maple-core pins. Groton employees tested the machines while enjoying lunch-hour bowling. The company later sold the technology to AMF, which revolutionized the sport with it.

ELCO FLORIDA UNIT, C. 1947. To broaden its sales base for its power cruisers, Elco opened Elco Cruisers, Inc., in Miami, Florida. Unfortunately, Elco's sales began sliding when the pleasure-cruiser market went soft and competition stiffened. In addition, Electric Boat in 1949 decided to concentrate on submarine production and Elco was closed, leaving an impressive legacy of yachts, many of which became collector's items.

MANAGEMENT GATHERING, 1948. Members of Electric Boat management gather for a group portrait. General manager O. Pomeroy Robinson Jr. is at the center of the first row. Other top executives include Dr. Andrew I. McKee, vice president of engineering (second from left, first row) and Frank N. Kelly, company treasurer (seated at far right, first row). Today the company has a management club.

ARMORLITE TRUCK BODIES, C. 1949. Truck bodies made of a lightweight, durable, and strong aluminum-magnesium material called Armorlite were one item the shipyard experimented with producing after the war. At first, prospects were encouraging, but failure to reach a satisfactory sales agreement with the trucking industry finally doomed the project, and the product was dropped.

BRIDGE CONSTRUCTION, C. 1949. Electric Boat fabricated the structural steel for this bridge and many others in the late 1940s. The work was performed at the shipyard, then the material was shipped to the construction sites by truck or rail. One such large project was fabricating the steel for the bridges on Connecticut's Wilbur Cross Parkway, named for the state's wartime governor.

OARSMEN, 1949. With the north yard steel craneways and the Groton shore behind them, the Electric Boat Athletic Club rowing crew poses on a pier after winning a race held on the Mystic River as part of the Stonington, Connecticut, tercentennial celebration. Rowing is no longer a sport in the athletic club, but thousands of members still gather for basketball, golf, and tennis tournaments each year.

CANADAIR HOCKEY TEAM, 1949. Canada has always been known for its devotion to the challenging sport of hockey, and this Canadair team met the challenge admirably. The team won the first-place trophy for the 1948–1949 season in the Montreal Industrial League. The team also led the league in the 1949–1950 season.

PRINTING PRESS PRODUCTION, C. 1950. Finding a good market for its Willard offset printing press, another nonmarine item developed after the war, Electric Boat set up a division in Groton to manufacture the product. Here presses come off the Printing Machinery Division's production line. The press was a high-speed unit capable of turning out top-quality full-color work at a rate of 4,000 to 6,000 impressions per hour. The division started delivering the presses in 1947 in the United States and also sold them in such foreign countries as neighboring Canada, and Switzerland, Portugal, New Zealand, Argentina, and India. Faced with intense competition in the postwar printing press industry, Electric Boat sold the operation to another company in the early 1950s. Shortly afterward, the yard began to give most of its attention to projects involving the emerging nuclear era.

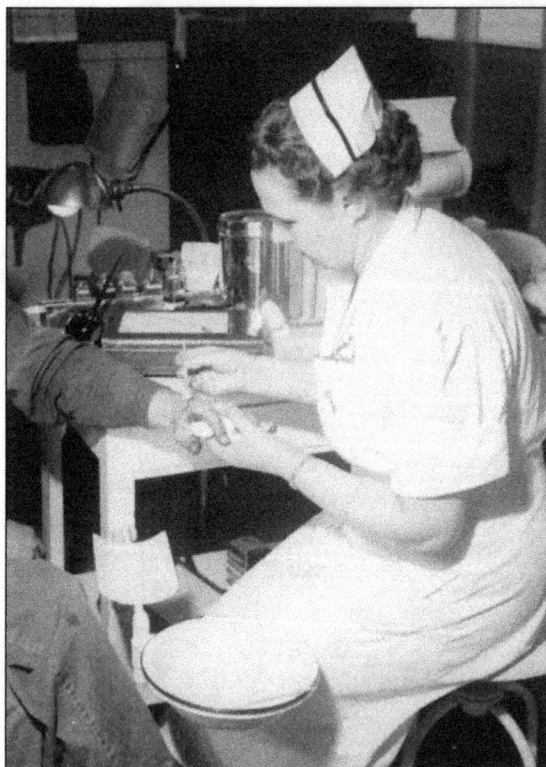

HOSPITAL NURSE TREATS EMPLOYEE, 1951. A nurse at the yard hospital attends to an employee's injured hand. The fully staffed two-story outpatient facility, managed by the company doctor, handles the primary medical needs of the Groton workforce, administering first aid, various kinds of tests, and other routine medical help when needed.

HUNTER-KILLER SUBMARINE, 1951. The diesel-powered *K-1*, built by Electric Boat in 1951 and the first American submarine designed from the keel up to seek out and destroy enemy submarines, cruises on Long Island Sound on its sea trials. The bulbous bow housed sophisticated sonar gear to track targets. The name was later changed to *Barracuda*. The shipyard built a total of three of these ships.

ADVANCED PT BOAT, 1951. After the war, Electric Boat continued its activity in the development of PT boats. Here a 98-foot descendant of the famed Elco 80-footers, built at Groton and delivered to the U.S. Navy in 1951, speeds along in a flat calm. To make it as light as possible, the hull and superstructure were constructed of riveted aluminum instead of the mahogany hull and molded plywood superstructure of its ancestors.

JOHN JAY HOPKINS (1893–1957). A former lawyer and assistant to the treasury secretary, John Hopkins joined Electric Boat as legal counsel and a director in 1937. Ten years later, as company president, he purchased the Canadian aircraft company Canadair as an Electric Boat subsidiary. In 1952, he founded General Dynamics Corporation with Electric Boat as the founding division. At his death in 1957, Electric Boat was the world leader in nuclear submarine technology.

CANADAIR PLANT, 1950. Canadair had two sprawling plants in Montreal near the Cartiersville Airport when Hopkins bought the organization on April 30, 1946. This image shows one of the two plants, which were producing four-engine DC-4-type transport planes and converting two-engine C-47 transport planes into DC-3 commercial airliners. On January 20, 1947, Canadair became a wholly owned subsidiary of Electric Boat.

CANADAIR FOUR IN FLIGHT, 1951. Canadair produced a number of these Canadair Four aircraft in both passenger and transport configurations in the late 1940s and early 1950s. The airplane's four engines generated 7,000 horsepower, which enabled an impressive level flight speed of 345 miles per hour and a range of 4,000 miles.

JETS ON THE ASSEMBLY LINE, 1951. F-86A Sabres, at that time the fastest jet fighter in the world, come together on the production line at a Canadair plant. At right, dozens of cockpit assemblies await their turn on the line. Canadair received an initial order for 100 of the airplanes in 1949 from the Royal Canadian Air Force and over the next few years built more than 1,800 of the sleek aircraft for the Royal Canadian Air Force, Colombia, South Africa, and West Germany. The F-86, designed and built in the United States by North American Aviation on Long Island, was the free world's premier jet fighter during the Korean War in the early 1950s. Many of them were flown by United Nations forces in the conflict and built up a good combat record battling their counterparts, Russian MiG fighters, in fierce aerial dogfights.

BRITANNIA FUSELAGE WORK, 1952. Workers install interior components in fuselage sections of the Bristol *Britannia* airliner at Canadair. That passenger airplane evolved into the CL-28, a maritime reconnaissance aircraft, the largest plane built in Canada to that date. The first CL-28 was delivered to the Royal Canadian Air Force in 1958. In 1976, to preserve Canada's independent aviation industry, the Canadian government bought Canadair from General Dynamics for $38.15 million.

YARD ROAD, C. 1952. This image, taken in early 1952, looks north along Electric Boat's main thoroughfare, which runs for the better part of a mile through the shipyard linking the north and south yards at Groton. The buildings on the left and right are storehouses. The machine shop appears in the distance in the center.

Six

THE NUCLEAR ERA

HISTORIC KEEL LAYING, 1952. Pres. Harry Truman initials the keel of the *Nautilus* at Groton's south yard on June 14, 1952. Looking on at Truman's right is John Jay Hopkins, president and founder of General Dynamics. Behind Truman is O. Pomeroy Robinson Jr., Electric Boat general manager. Navy Secretary Dan Kimball is at Truman's left. The ceremony marked the official start of construction of the world's first nuclear-powered ship. The *Nautilus* project was the largest ever undertaken by the shipyard to that time. Even before the keel laying, a growing Electric Boat workforce was busy designing and planning for the thousands of details that would go into the monumental effort. In fact, most employees by that time were engaged in some area of the *Nautilus* project, which propelled the company almost overnight into a position of technological leadership in nuclear propulsion and onto a new level of submarine technology.

CARLETON SHUGG (1899–1992), C. 1952. A 1920 graduate of the United States Naval Academy with a master's degree from the Massachusetts Institute of Technology, Carleton Shugg had been deputy general manager of the Atomic Energy Commission when he joined Electric Boat in 1952. As vice president of General Dynamics and Electric Boat Division general manager, Shugg led the company through its massive buildup and historic production in the early years of the nuclear era.

OLD LETTERING COMES OFF, 1952. A spectator on the ground looks on as workers begin taking off old lettering of New London Ship and Engine on the front of the main office building shortly after Electric Boat became the founding division of General Dynamics in 1952. Electric Boat remained a division of the corporation until 1993, when it became a wholly owned subsidiary after corporate structural changes.

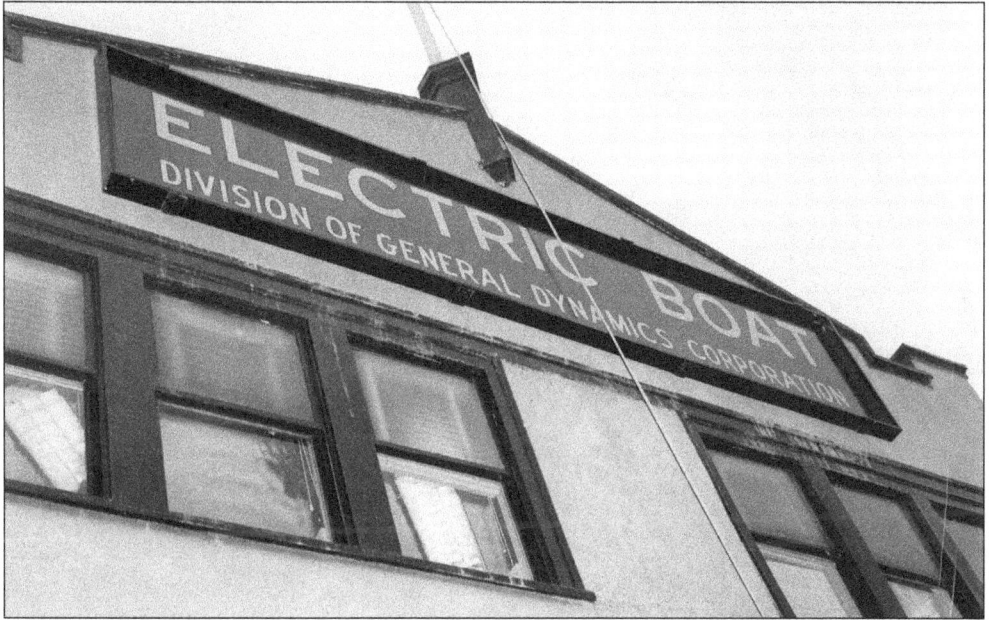

NEW LETTERING GOES ON, 1952. This name board showing the new affiliation covers the old Nelseco letters on the office building's facade. The name change brought some confusion, too. When telephone operators began answering calls with "Good morning, General Dynamics," callers would often hang up, thinking they had a wrong number. "Changing a firm's name is not a simple matter of relettering the front door," a company spokesman informed one newspaper.

VEHICLE LETTERING CHANGE, 1952. An Electric Boat sign painter puts finishing touches on truck lettering. Updating the vehicle fleet lettering was just one facet of the large name-change project. The change also affected logos, letterhead stationery, telephone books, and hundreds of company signs, which meant quantities of work for printers and sign painters.

DESIGN BUILDING GROUNDBREAKING, 1952. Andrew I. McKee, then director of research and design, breaks ground for a new design office building on November 24, 1952. Looking on are, from left to right, Gilbert May, excavation subcontractor's representative; Stephen Gardner, plant engineer; O. Pomeroy Robinson Jr., General Dynamics senior vice president; Carlton Shugg, general manager; and Thomas O'Shea, prime contractor's representative. The building was one of several built in the early 1950s.

ROBINSON RESEARCH BUILDING, 1952. In a view taken shortly after it opened, this building was named for O. Pomeroy Robinson Jr., longtime Electric Boat general manager. The facility was devoted to researching human and environmental factors, including submarine habitability, in the early years of nuclear submarine development. One important project was finding the most soothing color to paint the interior of the submarines.

NAUTILUS CONSTRUCTION PROGRESSES, 1953. As construction moves ahead swiftly, yard workers on staging and the submarine itself "deck over" the forward section of the *Nautilus* in the fall of 1953. The unfinished conning tower (left center) nearly reaches to the top of the craneway. The U.S. Navy's Underwater Sound Laboratory across the Thames River in New London appears in the background. Because the *Nautilus* was the most challenging project Electric Boat had undertaken to that time and the first platform in a revolutionary new area of propulsion, its construction received extra attention down to the last detail. Testing, checking, rechecking, and further testing were the order of the day throughout the endeavor. When it went to sea in 1955 for the first time (see page 105), the *Nautilus* was operating with the most sophisticated technology in naval and maritime history.

EMERGENCY POWER PRODUCERS, C. 1953. These five diesel generators, built by New London Ship and Engine Company, provided emergency and supplementary current for Electric Boat's Groton facility from the 1930s and well into the post–World War II era. For identification purposes, they were lightheartedly named by powerhouse workers after the famous Dionne quintuplets born in Canada in 1932.

GRINDING A WELD, 1953. A grinder takes down a weld on the port tailshaft fairing of the *Nautilus* during the final stages of construction. He had already performed the same work on the starboard tailshaft. The early nuclear submarines were twin-screwed, but a change in hull shape a few years later made single-screw propulsion more efficient and enabled greater speed.

SUBMARINE IN IDAHO, 1953. While the hull for the world's first nuclear-powered ship was coming together at Groton, Electric Boat craftsmen were installing the prototype nuclear reactor for the *Nautilus* at the Atomic Energy Commission's Arco, Idaho, testing station. The round tank simulated underwater conditions the *Nautilus* would encounter when operating.

NEW HANDLING SYSTEM, 1953. Workmen put the finishing touches on the diesel-powered target-training submarine *T-1* in 1953. The *T-1* and a sister ship, *T-2*, both built by Electric Boat, were fitted with a control system similar to those in aircraft so they could be operated by one man. Jointly developed by the company and the U.S. Navy, the system supplanted the traditional three-man submarine navigating crew—bow planesman, stern planesman, and helmsman.

HYMAN G. RICKOVER (1900–1986), C. 1954. Adm. Hyman G. Rickover (then a captain), a 1922 United States Naval Academy graduate known as the "Father of the Nuclear Navy," conceived the idea for nuclear propulsion for submarines and approached Electric Boat. O. Pomeroy Robinson Jr., Electric Boat general manager, agreed to build the *Nautilus* in 1951, opening a bright future for the firm. Admiral Rickover spent 63 years in the U.S. Navy, the longest naval career on record.

NAUTILUS CHRISTENING, 1954. "I christen thee *Nautilus*. May God bless her and all who sail in her." So spoke First Lady Mamie Eisenhower just before she smashed a traditional silver-encased bottle of champagne on the *Nautilus* (SSN 571) at the submarine's historic launching. Recalling the elegance of bygone days, Eisenhower arrived at the event on a private railroad car, which was backed into the yard.

NAUTILUS LAUNCHING, 1954. The *Nautilus* enters the Thames River precisely at 11:00 a.m. 'during its launching on January 21, 1954. As an omen of sorts, the sun burned off a thick fog 15 minutes before the ceremony. The event took on the trappings of a national holiday throughout the area. Schools and businesses were closed. Some 15,000 people crowded into the south yard for the historic occasion.

NAUTILUS JOINS THE FLEET, 1954. Some 1,200 spectators look on at an Electric Boat pier as the *Nautilus* is commissioned into the fleet on September 30, 1954. In this view, the crew, assembled on deck, and other naval personnel salute as the flag goes up on the staff aft of the conning tower (center right) to the strains of the national anthem played by the band at the upper right.

BARGE SECTION LIFT, 1954. Workers stand by to ease the first section of a new welded steel barge Electric Boat was building for its neighbor, the pharmaceutical firm Pfizer, which, since 1948, has occupied the site that was the victory yard during World War II. The 145-foot barge, delivered later that year, was used for transporting fermentation by-products.

SHIFT END EXODUS, 1954. As construction on the early nuclear submarine fleet increased, employment rose dramatically at Electric Boat, exceeding even World War II levels. Here thousands of workers stream up the south yard hill past the Robinson Research building at the end of the first shift heading for the time clocks adjacent to the south yard entrance. The same scene was playing out at the north yard hill. As during World War II, the company advertised throughout most of the country for experienced tradespeople to join the workforce. Electric Boat also set up trade training programs and enlarged the apprenticeship program that had been operating for years. In perhaps the best aspect of training, after classroom and practical training the trainees were teamed with experienced people. This procedure had worked well during the war before the opening of the victory yard. Well-trained employees had brought the yard to full production very quickly.

FIRST RAILWAY CUSTOMER, 1954. Sitting high, but not yet dry, the fleet-type submarine *Diablo* (SS 479), which arrived on August 19, 1954, for a routine overhaul, becomes the first boat hauled on the newly completed marine railway. The railway, with its wooden deck gleaming, replaced its antiquated predecessor, which had been constructed in 1923 just north of the north yard building ways to handle overhauls of the group of World War I S boats and later used for building and overhauling yachts and commercial vessels. While most crewmen gather on the *Diablo*'s deck to get a look at their new surroundings, two crewmen at left center secure a tall boarding ladder while yard workers stand by ready to lend a hand. The New London skyline serves as a backdrop for two cranes, a tugboat, and a submarine heading up the river.

HISTORIC NAUTILUS VOYAGE, 1955. The *Nautilus* heads to sea after leaving Electric Boat on January 21, 1955, radioing the famous message "Underway on nuclear power," which is overprinted on this image. The *Nautilus* went on the make the pages of Jules Verne come alive as an awed world watched, breaking all existing submarine speed and endurance records and transiting the polar ice cap from west to east submerged, capturing yet another first.

SEAWOLF LAUNCHING, 1955. The world's second nuclear submarine, the *Seawolf* (SSN 575) hits the water at Groton on July 25, 1955, from the south yard. General Electric designed and constructed the submarine's power plant prototype in a steel sphere at West Milton, New York. It was the first sodium-cooled reactor. The *Seawolf* set a new submerged endurance record of two months.

SLIDING OUT, 1955. In this unusual view, the stern of the *Seawolf* begins pushing up a wave as it slides into the Thames River at better than 20 miles per hour during its launching. Spectators in the area at left and atop the building behind them are obviously getting an exciting close-up view of the event.

FACE-LIFT FOR OFFICE BUILDING, C. 1955. Here is the main office building as it appeared in the mid-1950s. The building sports a new entryway and updated raised lettering General Dynamics Corporation Electric Boat Division high on the facade. The building contrasts sharply with the more modern nuclear engineering building, part of which appears at right.

LAST DIESEL SUBMARINE, 1956. The *Darter* (SS 576) was the last diesel submarine built by Electric Boat. It took shape in the mid-1950s alongside some intimidating cousins, the first nuclear submarines. The *Darter* went on to a distinguished 36-year career in the U.S. Navy as a symbol of a passing era in American naval history.

FIRST POLARIS SUBMARINE, 1958. Another first for Electric Boat and the country, the Polaris missile-firing *George Washington* (SSBN 598) fires a sabot, or dummy missile, at sea. The Polaris program was so urgent in the early cold war years that a nearly completed attack submarine at Groton was cut in half and a missile section added. Its sail is now on exhibit outside the Submarine Force Library and Museum in Groton.

Research Vessel, 1958. Electric Boat acquired this 290-ton oceanographic research vessel, the *Sea Surveyor*, early in 1958 and refitted it for physical and biological oceanography and underwater acoustic studies. The 118-foot ship was later equipped with a two-man deep-diving research submarine that was built by Electric Boat. The *Sea Surveyor* had a cruising range of 4,000 miles.

Arctic Pioneer, 1959. The *Skate* (SSN 578), the nation's third nuclear submarine, sits surfaced in the Arctic as three crew members check thick chunks of ice it broke through while coming up. The *Skate*, designed and built by Electric Boat, was the lead ship in the first class of nuclear submarines. It surfaced at the North Pole, the first submarine in history to do so, on March 17, 1959.

Triton Launch, 1958. The *Triton* (SSN 586), at 440 feet the longest American submarine built to that time, is launched on August 19, 1958. When waterborne, the *Triton* kept surging toward the opposite shore and had to be chased and stopped by tugs. Thereafter, all submarines launched at Groton carried large tethered cement blocks that were dropped shortly after launching. Submarines later dragged heavy chain to arrest postlaunch motion.

Meeting on the Thames, 1959. The *Triton* (left) and the *Skipjack* (SSN 585), built side by side at Electric Boat's south yard, meet in the Thames River off the shipyard. The *Triton*, the only submarine ever powered by two reactors, was much longer than the *Skipjack*, which, at 252 feet, was one of the smaller boats in the fleet. The *Triton* circumnavigated the world submerged in 1960, the first such voyage.

SKIPJACK UNDERWAY, 1959. With water coursing up over its forward deck and around its sail, the *Skipjack* (SSN 585) makes a tight turn to starboard. The attack submarine was the first mating of a whale-shaped hull and nuclear power. The result was the fastest submarine designed to that time. It was also the first nuclear-powered submarine to have a single screw. Up to that time, they were twin-screwed.

SUBMARINE HUNTER, 1960. The advanced hunter-killer nuclear submarine *Tullibee* (SSN 597) was the only one of its kind ever built. Delivered to the U.S. Navy by Electric Boat on November 9, 1960, and one of the smaller submarines in the fleet, it was basically an experimental platform for state-of-the-art submarine detection and tracking gear.

OLD AND NEW LOGOS, 1961.
Standing alongside a water tower carrying the General Dynamics symbol in this 1961 image, the smokestack recalled that the Groton plant was the New London Ship and Engine Company when first built 50 years earlier. Both structures were demolished in the early 1980s. The modern building in the background houses some of the company's design department offices and a plant cafeteria.

FIRST LADY ACCEPTS FLOWERS, 1979. First Lady Rosalynn Carter accepts a bouquet from the flower girl before initialing the keel of the Trident submarine *Georgia* (SSBN 729). Rosalynn, whose husband, Pres. Jimmy Carter, had served as an officer in the nuclear submarine force and had lived in Groton near Electric Boat when he was in submarine school, was a logical choice for the position. The *Georgia* was the third Trident submarine built by Electric Boat.

LAFAYETTE CHRISTENING, 1962. First Lady Jacqueline Kennedy christens the *Lafayette* (SSBN 616) on May 8, 1962, at Electric Boat's south yard. Looking on at right is Roger Lewis, then president of General Dynamics. The *Lafayette* was the lead vessel in a 32-ship class designed to fire the Polaris A-3 missile.

RESEARCH SUBMARINE ALUMINAUT, 1964. Electric Boat built the *Aluminaut*, the world's first aluminum submarine, for Reynolds International, Inc. The *Aluminaut* was 51 feet long, had a six-and-a-half-inch-thick pressure hull, and was powered by two five-horsepower electric motors, one for horizontal propulsion, the other for vertical propulsion. Carrying an operator and two observers, it could dive to 15,000 feet. It is now displayed at the Reynolds Museum in Richmond, Virginia.

DRAMATIC SURFACING, 1965. Looking like a broaching whale, the Electric Boat–built *Benjamin Franklin* (SSBN 640) sends white spray flying as it bursts to the surface. Delivered to the U.S. Navy on October 22, 1965, the *Franklin* was the lead ship in the first class designed to fire the Poseidon ballistic missile, successor to the Polaris missile.

THE STAR BOATS, 1966. The research submarines *Star II* (left) and *Star III*, built by Electric Boat in 1966, were operated as a commercial enterprise by the shipyard for several years and performed a variety of tasks in the collection of oceanographic data for public utilities, private industry, and the U.S. Navy. The 17-foot *Star II* could descend to 1,200 feet and the 24-foot *Star III* to 2,000 feet.

113

NR-1, 1969. With the Groton shore in the background and shepherded by a tug, the *NR-1*, the world's first and only nuclear-powered research submarine, heads up the Thames River after a trial run. Electric Boat delivered the tiny vessel to the U.S. Navy on October 27, 1969. Among other events, it was used in the recovery efforts after the space shuttle *Challenger* disaster in 1986.

ILLUSORY STERN VIEW, 1975. If not for the sail and diving planes far forward, this stern view of the Electric Boat–built fast-attack submarine *Glenard P. Lipscomb* might be mistaken for a whale gliding along on the surface. The object in the foreground, which looks like it might be the fluke of a tail, is actually the top of *Lipscomb*'s rudder.

THE GRISWOLD HOTEL, C. 1968. Groton's 400-room Griswold Hotel (center), built in the early 1900s by railroad magnate Morton Plant, who had an opulent summer home nearby, was the scene of many Electric Boat launching parties. The hotel for years was a mecca for wealthy vacationers who docked their yachts at the hotel's pier and played the 18-hole golf course behind the hotel. The Griswold Hotel was torn down in 1969.

WIRE WINDER AT ELECTRO DYNAMIC, 1976. Dolores Lee, a wire winder at the Electro Dynamic Company, feeds wire into a large electric motor at the subsidiary's plant in Avenel, New Jersey. The firm had moved from Bayonne after a fire destroyed its facility there. Later Electro Dynamic produced pipe hangers for nuclear submarines. The company closed the facility in 2000 because of a declining workload.

KEEL READIED FOR CEREMONY, 1976. The keel section for the first Trident missile–firing submarine, the *Ohio* (SSBN 726), a gigantic 48 feet in diameter, is lifted into position in Building 260, the yard's Groton assembly building, in preparation for formal keel-laying ceremonies. Planning for the photograph was not easy, but Joseph Wornom Jr., then Electric Boat's public relations manager, figured out an ingenious solution to comply with the U.S. Navy's long-standing security directive that the hull section thickness could not be shown in any photograph. Wornom had the section wrapped in plastic sheeting and had the image shot in silhouette so there was no chance of hull thickness appearing. Impressed, the U.S. Navy cleared the picture for release. The image, which received heavy media attention all over the world, heralded the start of construction of the largest submarines ever built in the United States.

PONTOON ARRIVAL, 1976. The 600-foot launch pontoon for the new land level construction facility arrives off Groton from Newburgh, New York, where it was built. As the tow rounded the battery at the tip of Manhattan, a passing tug skipper asked, "What's that thing you're towing?" "A pontoon," came the reply. The other skipper laughed. "If that's a pontoon, I'd like to see the airplane it goes on." (Author's collection.)

PONTOON DOCKS, 1976. Looking like a floating football field, the pontoon is eased against a wing wall to undergo final outfitting before being installed in the land level facility graving dock. The tug in the foreground is the *Kingston II*, built of scrap submarine steel by welder apprentices in 1937. After a 39-year yard career, it was donated to Mystic Seaport, where it moves the museum's exhibit ships. (Author's collection.)

PONTOON INSTALLED, 1976. With tugs assisting, the pontoon is eased into the graving dock. Clearance was a scant four inches on each side. In the launching process, a submarine is moved onto it, the dock is emptied, and the pontoon rests on the dock's bottom. Then the dock and pontoon are flooded, and the submarine floats free. The dock contains 37 million gallons of water when flooded. (Author's collection.)

HOMEWARD BOUND, 1977. First-shift employees pour out of the shipyard main gate (upper right) onto Eastern Point Road in Groton after another day of work. Some head for the buses parked at left that provided transportation to satellite parking lots and some neighboring communities. The nuclear engineering building appears at left, and a multilevel parking building at right. To boost the workforce in the early years of the nuclear era, Electric Boat had embarked upon the largest recruiting program in its history, with a heavy print advertising campaign in newspapers all over the country. The advertisements called for both tradespeople and white-collar workers. As during World War II, the company set up trade training programs. All the training included advanced techniques, including nuclear welding, which would become a leading yard discipline. In the late 1970s, employment reached more than 25,000, then peaked at 27,000 in the 1980s.

NEW TRUCK, 1977. Electric Boat firemen look over a new emergency truck in front of the plant's fire department. At left inside the building are a fire truck and an ambulance. The company has a fully staffed fire department trained in all types of shipyard fires as well as structure fires and serves as a backup unit for the Groton Fire Department when needed.

MAJOR QUONSET FACILITY, 1978. This aerial view shows Electric Boat's Quonset Point, Rhode Island, facility. The large white building in the center is the $110 million Automated Submarine Frame and Cylinder Manufacturing facility, which was built in 1978. Support buildings are at the lower right and to the building's left. Narragansett Bay appears at the upper right.

AUTOMATED HULL MACHINE, 1978. This massive Automated Frame and Cylinder Manufacturing machine inside the building appearing in the bottom image on page 119 speeds the construction of submarine frames and cylinders and saves manufacturing and labor costs. The huge ring-shaped frame mounted on the legs to either side can be turned to enable automated welding on hull sections. When the welding is completed, interior hull components are installed at Quonset Point, allowing faster joining with other hull sections in the modular (sectional) construction system used at Groton. Before this innovative system, interior hull components were installed during hull assembly at the shipyard, slowing the construction process considerably. The completed hull sections make the 40-mile trip to the Groton shipyard by water on a specially designed barge, the *Sea Shuttle*, (see top image on the opposite page) where they are joined together to form completed ships.

DEDICATED BARGE, 1979. The *Sea Shuttle*, the barge designed from the keel up for the task, carries hull sections from Quonset Point to Groton. The three large jacking legs, similar to those on oil rigs, permit the barge to be positioned precisely and held in place at piers when loading or unloading cargo regardless of the height of the tide.

COMPANY HOUSE FLAG, 1978. Electric Boat's house flag has this color scheme: a background field of dark blue, sub silhouette of light blue, and oval stripe of white, and black General Dynamics letters. The design was the winner in a 1978 contest open to all employees at the Groton shipyard that drew 1,700 entries. First prize was a $1,000 U.S. savings bond, which was won by a clerk at the yard.

SPECTATORS AT LAUNCHING, 1978. Thousands of employees and their families watch as the 360-foot fast-attack submarine *Bremerton* (SSN 698), crew at attention on sail planes and deck, enters the Thames River during its launching at Groton on July 22, 1978. Electric Boat built 33 of the 61 ships in the class, which played a deadly game of cat-and-mouse with Russian ships during the last third of the cold war.

OHIO DEBUT, 1978. With a large construction jig still in place on its bow section, the *Ohio*, the first Trident submarine, sits on the land level facility platform after being moved out of the assembly building at rear where it was built. The towering submarine, seven stories high, dwarfs yard workers at the lower right.

MULTI-WHEELED TRANSPORTER, 1979. A huge 700-ton-capacity multi-wheeled transporter moves a hull section off-loaded from the *Sea Shuttle* to the assembly building at Groton. The strange-looking vehicle's tiny operator's cab (right) is almost hidden under the carrying platform. The most frequently asked question from curious onlookers is "What do you do when one of the inside tires goes flat?" The transporter was replaced later by an even large one.

CONVENTION BOOTH, C. 1980. In this early-1980s image, Electric Boat graphics manager Vincent Malcolm (right), discusses a large photograph at the company's exhibit booth at one of the several military organization conventions in which Electric Boat participates each year. Models of Trident (the larger one) and Los Angeles–class fast-attack submarines, which the company was producing at that time, are at Malcolm's right on the exhibit counter.

WINNING RAFT CREW, 1980. The winning crew and project support people pose proudly for the photographer after winning the local Annual Sailfest Festival raft race on the Thames River. The challenge was building a raft without attaching any parts with nails or screws. The team took the finish gun with a fiberglass catamaran propelled by oars and a sail. The company participates in many such community events.

BOW DECORATION, 1985. After nuclear submarines were built with whale-shaped hulls, sign painters at Electric Boat crafted canvas decorations to go over the bow for each launching. This one was for the *Pittsburgh* (SSN 720), a Los Angeles–class fast-attack submarine launched on November 23, 1985. All the submarines in that class were named for American cities except one, the *Hyman G. Rickover* (SSN 709).

LAND LEVEL FACILITY, 1979. In this aerial view of the land level submarine construction facility, spectators watch launching of the fast-attack submarine *Phoenix* (SSN 702) on December 8, 1979. Two Trident submarines tower over the spectators, and a third sits in the graving dock at right. Covering several acres, the facility is constructed of cells made of 62 miles of sheet piling filled with 16,000 truckloads of sand and gravel.

TECHNOLOGY CENTER, 1985. The Electric Boat Technology Center appears shortly after its opening in 1985. The 10-story structure was the first office building built in decades at the facility and supplanted the old office building as the administrative hub. The vertical tower in the building's center are elevator shafts.. The smaller building in the foreground housed the security department and is a visitor entrance.

TRIDENT UNDERWAY, 1986. The Trident submarine *Nevada* (SSBN 733) churns the Atlantic Ocean into a froth on its sea trials. The 560-foot submarine, manned on alternate 90-day patrols by either the "Blue" or "Gold" crews of 154 men each, is one of the entire fleet of 18 designed and built for the U.S. Navy by Electric Boat from the 1970s into the 1990s.

TRIDENT AWAITS CHRISTENING, 1989. With bunting in place, another Trident submarine, the *West Virginia* (SSBN 736), floats in the land level facility graving dock ready for its christening. To its left is a sister ship under construction. The *West Virginia* was delivered to the U.S. Navy on October 20, 1990. All Tridents were named for states except the *Henry M. Jackson* (SSBN 730), which honored the Michigan senator.

SEAWOLF AT SEA, 1995. The first in an interim class of fast-attack submarine, the *Seawolf* (SSN 21), was launched on June 24, 1995. Electric Boat has since delivered all three ships in the class, which includes the *Connecticut* (SSN 22) and the *Jimmy Carter* (SSN 23). The first two ships displace 9,137 tons and are 353 feet long, while the heavily modified *Carter* is 453 feet long.

NEWEST SUBMARINE, 2004. The nation's newest submarine, the *Virginia* (SSN 774), built by Electric Boat, joined the fleet on October 12, 2004. It is the first ship in a new class of attack submarine designed to be the quietest ever. In another innovation, the reactor produces power for the lifetime of the ship, eliminating the need for refueling. The *Virginia* displaces 7,700 tons and is 377 feet long.

Visit us at
arcadiapublishing.com

www.ingramcontent.com/pod-product-compliance
Lightning Source LLC
Chambersburg PA
CBHW080626110426
42813CB00006B/1615

* 9 7 8 1 5 3 1 6 2 7 9 9 7 *